D0651249

The Pastor
and
Vocational
Counseling

The Pastor
and
Vocational
Counseling

by

Charles F. Kemp

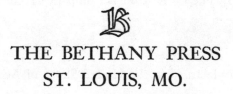

THE BETHANY PRESS
ST. LOUIS, MO.

Copyright © 1961
by
THE BETHANY PRESS

Library of Congress Catalog Card No. 61-8602

Distributed in Australasia
by the Austral Printing and Publishing Company, Melbourne,
and in Canada
by The G. R. Welch Company, Toronto

Manufactured in the United States of America

OVERTON MEMORIAL LIBRARY
HERITAGE CHRISTIAN UNIVERSITY
P.O. Box HCU
Florence, Alabama 35630

To

Elmer D. Henson, Dean Brite College
of the Bible, Texas Christian University
Fort Worth, Texas

Acknowledgments

I should like to take this opportunity to express my appreciation to Dr. Hoyt Williams, of the School of Education, Texas Christian University, Fort Worth, Texas, and to Dr. John Drakeford, of Southwestern Baptist Theological Seminary, also in Fort Worth, who were kind enough to read the manuscript in its entirety and make many helpful suggestions.

Contents

Introduction
The Significance of Vocational Choice and
    Adjustment   11

Part I. An Interpretation of the Vocational
    Guidance Movement

I.   Principles of Vocational Guidance   21
II.   History of Vocational Guidance   35
III.   Basic Techniques of Vocational Guidance:
    The Interview and Testing   53
IV.   Basic Techniques of Vocational Guidance:
    Occupational Information and Referral   73

Part II. The Minister and Vocational Counseling

V.   The Minister and Vocational Guidance   91
VI.   The Minister Counseling on Problems of Voca-
    tional Adjustment   101
VII.   Guidance for Church Vocations   115
VIII.   The Minister and Special Areas of Vocational
    Guidance   135

Appendixes

Appendix I.   A Chronological Chart of the Develop-
    ment of the Vocational Guidance
    Movement   165

Appendix II.   Quotations on the Theological Interpretation of Vocation   171

Appendix III. Sources of Referral on Vocational
Problems   181

Bibliography   183

Index   187

Introduction

THE SIGNIFICANCE OF
VOCATIONAL CHOICE AND
AN ADJUSTMENT

One of the most important and far-reaching decisions anyone is called upon to make is the choice of a life vocation. A man's vocational adjustment is of utmost importance. There are at least nine reasons why this is so.

(1) Choice of a vocation is important for practical economic reasons.

This is first on the list not because it is the most important but because it is the most obvious. In our culture a man is expected to provide a living for himself and his family. The problems of unemployment and inadequate income are too common to need elaboration. The standard of living of a man and his family, and his freedom from financial concern are determined to a large extent by his vocational choice.

(2) It is important because it determines a person's way of life.

There is an old saying that "making a life is more important than making a living." There is one sense in which this is true. Everyone would agree that the quality of one's life is more important than the size of his income. There is another sense in which the statement is misleading. It implies that there is a separation between the two—the fact is that, to

11

a large extent, the way one makes his living determines his way of life. When a man chooses a vocation, he also chooses a way of life.

A man's vocation is one of the most absorbing things of his life. It not only concerns a major portion of his day but it also influences what he thinks about and what he talks about the rest of the day. The people he associates with, the clothes he wears, the place he lives are largely determined by the job he does. There are no ranchers in New York City; there are few psychiatrists in country towns.

A man's role in society is determined by the job he does. His friends and associates will greet him differently, will have a different concept of him as a person if he is a preacher than if he were a football coach, the president of a bank, or a bartender. His status, his place in the community are strongly influenced by his vocation.

(3) Vocation is important because it influences a person's family life.

Everyone recognizes the importance of the home; educators, psychiatrists, psychologists, sociologists, ministers, judges are all stressing the significance of the home. Vocational life has a tremendous influence on family life—a fact that is often overlooked. Young women should recognize that their home life will be vastly different depending upon whether they marry a school teacher, a farmer, an airplane pilot, or a medical missionary. The atmosphere of the home, the relationships within the family, the place of the home in the community are largely determined by the nature of the occupation of one or both members of the marriage, whether or not the vocation is one which provides security and one in which all members of the family take pride and find satisfaction.

(4) It is important because a man's happiness depends upon it.

Pleasure is not, of course, the main end of life, yet happiness is something all men desire. The Declaration of Independence states that we have the right to life, liberty, and the pursuit of happiness. A man's work has a close relationship to this matter. That person who has found a vocation that he really enjoys, who is challenged by his work, who goes to his daily task with enthusiasm and interest is most fortunate. He has one of the primary requirements for a happy life. President Eliot of Harvard used to say that Harvard paid him for doing the very things he would gladly have done for nothing if it had been necessary. This is a description of a person who really enjoys his work and such an attitude leads to satisfaction in all areas of life.

On the other hand, that person whose job offers no challenge, who goes to his task each day with little interest and no enthusiasm or with a definite feeling of boredom or dislike has a problem which will in turn, influence his entire outlook.

(5) A man's vocation is important because his psychological and emotional well-being depend upon it.

Michelangelo is quoted as saying, "It is well with me only when there is a chisel in my hand." There is a new term in medical language, "occupational therapy." Strange as it would sound to some of our pioneer ancestors, there is a healing power in work. This has been found especially true in such places as mental hospitals and veterans' hospitals. Even weaving a basket can do much for a patient's outlook. When Richard Cabot, famous physician of Boston, wrote his classical little book, *What Men Live By*, he divided it into four points: work, play, love, and worship. These, he said, are the things men find necessary if life is to have value. It is significant that a physician would list worship last. It is also significant that he would say that the first thing is work.

(6) It is important because one's vocation does much to determine the meaning one finds in life.

That life has to have meaning is stressed by psychologists and theologians alike, and rightfully so. Every man has to have something that gives him a sense of value, a sense of significance, a sense of worth.

A man's sense of significance, his sense of worth is closely identified with the work he does. If he feels the work is worth while, that the work has value, then he has a sense of value too.

(7) Choice of a vocation is important because it is through his vocation that man makes one of his major contributions to society.

One of the great needs of our day is people who are committed to the service of mankind, people who are dedicated to the common good. In this respect the importance of vocational choice is not only an individual matter but one that is important to society as well. Every year thousands of young people leave school and enter the vocational world. In a world of such great moral and spiritual needs it is highly important that they find places where they can render their best and most needed service.

This is also true individually. There is no greater satisfaction in life than to be able to say: "My life counts, my efforts are worth while, the thing that I do is important." The one whose job consists only of earning enough money to purchase the necessities and some of the luxuries of life is denied one of life's greatest satisfactions, the satisfaction of saying, "I have made a real contribution; I have rendered a significant service."

(8) It is important because it influences one's attitude toward one's self.

Psychologically speaking, a man's concept of himself is

extremely important. A man's choice of a vocation is, in essence, a part of his concept of himself. He is saying, "I am a teacher, a statesman, a businessman, a farmer, a preacher." If this is something he can say with pride and satisfaction, then his sense of worth and self-acceptance is greatly re-enforced. If he cannot, then it is weakened.

One of the tragedies of unemployment is the feeling of inadequacy that accompanies it. The psychological accompaniments of unemployment, the sense of uselessness, are quite as real and can be just as serious as the economic ones. Someone else will feed the family of the unemployed man, but no one else can give him self-respect. This he must earn himself.

(9) Vocational choice is important because it is a religious matter.

This is a fact that has not been stressed by either the experts in vocational guidance or by theologians—but it is still true and may be the most significant point of all.

If God is concerned about all of life, then he is concerned about the way a man uses the time, the talents, and the abilities that have been entrusted to him. As one man put it, "God is as concerned about what happens between Sundays as he is about what happens on Sunday mornings." If this is true, then God is concerned about a man's vocational choice, the manner in which he conducts his vocational life and the contribution he makes through it. Thus the whole question of vocation becomes basically a religious question. A man's theology as well as his economic well-being are involved. Luther recognized this a long time ago. He saw every vocation as a "calling." It is only recently that theologians have again begun to rediscover the original meaning of a "vocation" as a "calling."

The place of the pastor in this total picture is apparent. He is concerned because he is concerned with persons; many of them bring their problems to him. Anything that has a widespread influence upon their lives is of interest to him. He is concerned because he is concerned about society. He is concerned because basically vocation is a religious matter and therefore touches his area of special responsibility.

How the pastor and the church can play a more effective role in helping people in their vocational lives is the subject of this volume.

Plan and Purpose of this Book

This book has been prepared primarily for the ministry, that is, pastors of local churches, directors of religious education, youth workers, university chaplains, chaplains in the armed services—all those who may be called upon to help someone with a problem of vocational choice or adjustment.

The book is divided into two main parts. The first part is an attempt to provide for the pastor an interpretation of the vocational guidance movement by discussing the general principles of vocational guidance, by tracing the main features of its historic development, and by outlining the basic techniques that are used.

The second part of the book deals with the work of the pastor as such. It is in no wise an attempt to make him into a vocational counselor; rather, it endeavors to point out both his opportunities and his limitations and to help him see the significance of the whole field and his unique relationship to it. Part I is primarily a background for Part II. Only as he understands something of the basic principles discovered in the vocational guidance movement can the pastor apply them to his own work.

This book was not written primarily for professional vocational counselors. Those who are trained in this field will recognize that much of the material in Part I is found in many volumes on vocational guidance. It is included here because pastors as a rule do not read books on vocational guidance; in fact, even the books on pastoral counseling refer to vocational guidance only occasionally and many of them do not mention it at all.

It is the hope of the author that Part II may have some value for the vocational counselor, that it might make him aware of the pastor's interest and of the contributions that a pastor can make, thus leading to closer co-operation.

This book is only introductory in nature. Much more needs to be done. This is a significant area that deserves every pastor's attention but hitherto it has been largely neglected.

Part I

An Interpretation
of the
Vocational Guidance Movement

I

PRINCIPLES OF VOCATIONAL
GUIDANCE

Vocational guidance takes place in many situations and is shared by many people. Teachers, counselors, psychologists, "Y" secretaries, social workers, employers, pastors, church school teachers, relatives, parents, friends—at some time or another all may participate in vocational guidance. This is inevitable. Whenever one person discusses with another a question or a problem of vocational choice, then, to some degree, vocational guidance takes place. With many this is vocational guidance of an informal type that is done as a part of, and almost incidental to, their other responsibilities. There are others for whom vocational guidance is a career. They are the specialists in the field.

The whole subject of vocational guidance has received increasing attention in recent years; in fact, we can rightfully say that vocational guidance has reached the proportions of a movement. We shall trace some of the chief features of the historical development of this movement in the next chapter. We shall see how it has developed a vast literature, conducted extensive research, and enlisted thousands of participants. One who is interested in vocational guidance in any capacity should know something of its background and some of the persons who have made outstanding contributions to its development. First, however, we shall list some basic principles that have grown out of the movement and that would be characteristic of the best vocational guidance today.

Vocational Guidance Deals with Normal People

When we speak of vocational guidance or vocational problems, we are speaking of normal problems of normal people. The person who is extremely disturbed emotionally or mentally sick has vocational problems too—very real ones—and they need to be faced. However, this is the kind of situation that must be dealt with by the physician and the psychiatrist. Once the emotional problem has been worked through, a vocational counselor can be of real assistance in helping this person find himself vocationally which is a real help in rehabilitation. In our discussion we are speaking of those who do have vocational problems but are normal people. They may be confused, discouraged, upset—they are not sick but they do need help.

Of course, there are some who would say that any difficulty in occupational choice or in occupational dissatisfaction is a sign of an emotional problem and to work with a specific matter such as a vocational problem is treating only a symptom. To this Herbert Sanderson replies "At the risk of oversimplification, it should be remembered that one need not take the entire automobile apart in order to change the spark plugs."[1]

To continue the analogy we might add that changing the spark plugs on a car that is otherwise in good condition will enable it to run much more smoothly and effectively.

[1] Sanderson, *Basic Concepts in Vocational Guidance* (New York: McGraw-Hill Book Company, Inc., 1954), p. 22. Used by permission.

Vocational Choice Cannot Be Separated from Other Aspects of Life

In one sense there is no such thing as vocational guidance per se; that is, vocational choice, or vocational adjustment is always tied up with personal, family, educational matters. At times there may be ethical or spiritual considerations; many factors operate in vocational choice such as status needs, personal drives and feelings, interpersonal influences and pressures.

In fact, Dr. Sanderson objects to the use of the term vocational guidance on the grounds that a discussion of one's vocational choice is never limited to a discussion of vocation alone and cannot realistically be separated from the rest of life. Then he uses the term in the title of his book because he can find none better. The fact remains, interrelated with other things though it is, there still is such a thing as vocational guidance.[2]

The whole person chooses a vocation and the whole person goes to work, not just a part of him. Because this is true, we should never assume that because a person comes seeking vocational guidance, this necessarily means that this is his only concern or even his major one.

Here, for example, is a young man considering the ministry. He goes to his pastor to discuss the problem. In the course of the conversation he says, "Now about my girl." Then he reveals the problem that his fiancée is not interested in becoming a minister's wife. This is a real problem. What is his primary concern—is it vocational, personal, premarital? Of course, it is all three.

Here is a young woman seeking help regarding what she

2 *Ibid.*, p. 7.

terms a vocational problem. She asks the counselor whether or not she ought to quit her job. Further discussion reveals that she is married; she supported her husband through four years of college and in the course of the four years she was advanced to a well-paying position. Now he is through school, has his own position but is not making as much money as she is. As a result, trouble has developed between them. There is a difficulty in communication, embarrassing things are said in front of friends. She feels it is because of her job. Is this a vocational problem? Obviously it has vocational factors but it also has other factors that have to do with their marriage relationship, with their understanding of masculine and feminine roles, and so forth.

At times a vocational counselor may begin by discussing a simple matter of vocational indecision and find he is in the midst of an interfamily conflict. For example, here is the boy who can't decide between law and teaching. This seems simple enough. On the surface he needs only to take some aptitude tests, consider what he wants to do the most, and make a decision. But it isn't that simple. The boy's father is a lawyer, his uncle is a lawyer, and everybody has taken it for granted he will be a lawyer—but he doesn't want to be a lawyer. The vocational problem cannot be resolved until the family situation is untangled.

At times adolescents may feel guilty because of these conflicts with their parents. Here is a boy who says, "Gosh, I'm just an ordinary boy—I don't know what I should be, but my folks keep after me all the time. They look at me and say, 'You're big enough to be deciding what you want to do—do you want to be a doctor or an engineer or what? I guess I am big enough but I still don't know."

At times an adolescent may express real hostility toward a parent over a conflict about vocational choice.

Such young people need help, not only with the matter of

vocational choice but also with their relationships with their families and with their attitudes toward themselves.

Where vocational problems are a part of other problems, the counselor deals with the whole person. Sometimes when the other factors are alleviated, the vocational problem is relieved also; but this is not always the case. The young person whose relationship with his family or fiancée complicates his vocational choice still faces the decision of finding the right choice for himself when his other problems have been solved.

Vocational Choice Includes a Concept of "Self"

One of the most important psychological facts about a person is his concept of himself. A person's concept of himself determines largely his motivation in life, to a great extent his behavior, and ultimately his adjustment and satisfaction in life. It includes many things: his feelings, hopes, ideals, goals, ambitions, previous experience—every thing, in fact, including his vocation.

When a person asks such questions as: "Who am I?" "What are my ambitions in life?" "What is my place in the world?" "What is the significance of my life?" he is asking questions that have to do with his concept of himself.

Donald E. Super says in the *Psychology of Careers:*

According to the self-concept theory, the occupation preferred should be one in which the individual expects to be able to be the kind of person he perceives himself as being, to assume a role which is congenial and compatible with the self concept.[3]

A person has a different concept of himself if he says, "I am a doctor," or "a farmer," or "a banker," or "an airplane pilot," or "a missionary."

[3] Super, *The Psychology of Careers* (New York: Harper & Brothers, 1957), p. 232. Used by permission.

Vocational Choice Can Be Made Only if One Understands Oneself

This is basic. Only as a person understands himself can he make an intelligent decision as to what he should do with his life. This includes his strengths and his weaknesses, his limitations and possibilities, his interests and his desires, his hopes and his fears. Most techniques of vocational guidance are designed for this purpose—to help a person gain an understanding of his abilities, his aptitudes, his interests, and his personality structure.

Actually this understanding of self is much deeper than anything that can be caught in a test. It goes back to the previous principle of gaining an understanding of one's concept of himself. No one can do it completely—life is too complex for that—but he can do much. This is the task of the counselor: not to diagnose and describe a person's attributes to him, but to help him gain insight into his own feelings, to help him gain a realistic and wholesome understanding of himself. This is far more difficult than measuring a few abilities and aptitudes and then telling him what he ought to do.

Vocational Choice Can Be Made Only if One Understands the Nature of the Vocation

It is surprising how many young people make a decision for a vocation without really knowing what is involved: the nature of the task, the training required, the anticipated earnings, and the more subtle factors such as the kind of life one will live if he makes such a decision.

Many choose vocations because of the glamor associated with the occupation, or because it is in line with their desire to move upward in the social scale (this may not even be conscious) or because of the influence of family or some admired friend or relative instead of on the basis of accurate and realistic information about the vocation itself.

However, ours is a very complicated world in which there are more than 20,000 different ways of making a living. A wise choice of one of these occupations can be made only when one has a full knowledge of the nature of the occupation. This includes thorough, accurate, and contemporary information about the opportunities and possibilities that are available. One study of the interests of high school youth showed that 61.7% were interested in entering the professional field but at the time of this study only 4.4% of the labor force were employed in the professional field. Only 8.8% were interested in agriculture and the mechanical arts but 61.1% of the population are engaged in agriculture or the mechanical arts.[4] Other studies show different percentages but similar results. This is what vocational counselors call "occupational information" and will be discussed at some length in the section on techniques.

Vocational Guidance and Eductional Guidance Are Inseparable

Vocational guidance is more than assisting a person in making the proper choice of an occupational or vocational field. It pertains also to the preparation and training for it, which includes selecting the proper schools, courses, curriculum, and so forth. Mistakes here can result in the loss of much time and money and may handicap a person in his whole vocational life and limit his contribution to society.

One who enters the vocational counseling field must be

---

[4] Cf. John E. Horrocks, *The Psychology of Adolescence* (Cambridge: The Riverside Press, 1951), p. 505.

familiar with academic procedures, educational requirements, and the whole learning process. Actually educational guidance is a specialty within itself. It includes such matters as appraising a person's abilities, an understanding of the educational requirements of a variety of occupations, motivation, over-achievement, underachievement, developing suitable educational plans. Just such a matter as choosing the proper college can be one that requires considerable time and understanding. For some this is easy. For others it is difficult. It requires the facing of such questions as: "Where are the best facilities available?" "What schools offer what I want?" "Should I stay at home or go away to school?" "What is the expense involved?" "Are scholarships available?" "Can I be accepted?" "What are my chances of graduating?" "What are the relative advantages of a state university, a church-related college, or a municipal university?" Young people need help with such questions. Their vocational future is determined largely by the nature and the quality of their education.

Vocational Choice Is Different at Different Levels of Maturity

In *The Psychology of Careers*, Donald Super includes a chapter entitled "Career Patterns and Life Stages." He draws on Charlotte Buehler's description of life stages which are five in number; the Growth Stage, the Exploratory Stage, the Establishment Stage, the Maintenance Stage, and the Decline. These life stages involve all aspects of life and living but Super relates them specifically to vocational selection and adjustment.

The Growth Stage extends from birth to about fourteen years. During this time the individual lives somewhat in a world of imagination and memory in which he speaks of being a policeman, a fireman, a cowboy, or other roles as a part of his play life.

The Exploratory Stage which runs roughly from 15 to about 25 depending on various factors such as length of schooling and so forth, is the period usually defined as adolescence. This is the period of growing up. There is often considerable floundering vocationally and otherwise. A typical high school student will select and discard six or eight occupations while he is in school; many do so in college even after some time may have been spent in preparation. This is the period when the young person is attempting to find out what constitutes adult behavior, what roles he wants to accept in life which includes his vocational plans and selections. As stated earlier, this is all a part of his attempt to develop a realistic concept of himself.

The Establishment Stage includes the years from twenty-five to forty-five. This is no longer the period of trial and error, of exploration. This is the time when one becomes established and plans for advancement, it is a period of hard work and effort.

The Maintenance Stage extends from about forty-five to sixty-five or retirement. By now a person has made his place in the vocational world, whatever the place may be—one of security or failure. In the vast majority of cases he does not attempt to break new ground, to establish new patterns. In many cases his creativity period is over, although there are some noteworthy exceptions. As Super points out, this stage can be one of fruition or frustration.

The final stage which is called one of Decline is divided into two sections: one the period of tapering off, of preparing for retirement, and the other of retirement itself with the adjustments that are necessary there.

Of course the age limits are very flexible. Some are still exploring possibilities in their fifties, some don't get established until late in life and some reach this stage by the twenties. Nevertheless, the process is one most persons go through.

The counselor needs to recognize this fact. Floundering in vocational matters in the adolescent is a normal and at times valuable fact. It is through such a process that he is testing reality, so to speak, and finding the real place for himself. After all, two thirds of the high school population change vocational plans while in school. Floundering for a man in his forties who cannot settle in a career or cannot get established is quite another factor.

Not to recognize this process and push a vocational choice too fast is a mistake. Many young people are hurried into premature vocational decisions. Schools urge them to reach a decision, speakers at career days stress it, their friends are announcing their decisions, their parents may be pressuring them so that they may make a choice simply because they feel they have to or because they are made to feel guilty if they do not, or simply to relieve some of the pressure others have placed on them rather than on a basis of what they really want to do or are fitted to do.

Vocational Choice Must Be Related to Ability

Anyone who would work in the field of vocational guidance must take into account the mental abilities of those with whom he works. This seems like a truism and it is for the vocational counselor; yet many others, such as pastors or friends who often give counsel or advice on vocations, do so without any accurate information about a person's intellectual ability or on occasion without even considering its importance. Yet one authority says, "The most important *single criterion* of an individual's ability to succeed or fail in any given occupational endeavor seems to be level of mental ability."[5]

The simple fact of the matter is that if a person finds himself in an occupation or a position that requires more ability than he possesses, he is not only doomed to vocational failure but to an embarrassing, frustrating, discouraging personal experience as well. On the other hand, if he selects a vocation that does not challenge or utilize all of the abilities he possesses, he is not only dissatisfied with his work but finds that life does not offer him the challenge that it should, and from a wider perspective, he is not making the creative contribution to society that he could.

Many mistakes are made at this point. Many studies of this problem have been made and they reach a common conclusion. Young people very commonly choose vocations that are above or below the level of their mental ability. One such study of 2,700 high school students found that 25% of the boys who listed the professions as their vocational choice had IQ's lower than is required for college entrance or success.[6]

This does not mean to imply that ability is the only factor that is important for vocational success or satisfaction. Far from it; it is only one factor. High ability does not indicate that one will succeed. He may not. It does indicate whether or not he has the capacity to secure the necessary training and do the work.

On the other hand, low ability is a good indication that he will not succeed. If a boy lists becoming a lawyer or a doctor as his ambition but has an IQ of 91 or 92, the chances that he can succeed are almost nil.

[5] *Ibid.*, p. 500.
[6] Cf. *Ibid.*, p. 502.

Vocational Guidance Must Take into Account the Feelings of the Individual

Not only the ability but the feelings of the person must be considered. This is true of all counseling, but is most likely to be overlooked in vocational counseling. In vocational guidance it is so easy to become involved in evaluating jobs, their nature, and opportunity and in looking at a person's abilities and aptitudes that his feelings about the whole experience may be slighted.

Vocational choice and adjustment come very easy for some. They may never have had a struggle with a decision, the entrance into the responsibilities of a vocational life may come quite naturally. For others it may be quite different. Some go through a period of great uncertainty. They suffer tremendous feelings of inadequacy and insecurity. Their decision may be complicated by family pressures or be loaded with attitudes of fear, even guilt. For some it is fraught with disappointments; many are forced to take second choices or they do not gain admission to the professional school they desired and are forced to change their plans. Such experiences may result in feelings of failure or worthlessness.

Ruth Strang illustrates the results of pressure on an eighteen-year-old girl who wrote:

Trying to decide on a permanent goal in life has caused me more serious mental distress than anything else I know of. To make things worse, my sister who is fifteen months younger than I, decided once and for all that she wanted to enter nurse's training. My mother thought there was something lacking in me as I would change from one plan to another, with no apparent reason or sense. I am inclined to think that something could be wrong with me because I want to do too many things in life.[7]

[7] Strang, *The Adolescent Views Himself* (New York: McGraw-Hill Book Company, Inc., 1957), p. 413. Used by permission.

Vocational guidance of this girl would be quite different from that of another student who has known from childhood that he wanted to go into his father's business. In fact, one might almost say that to understand and accept the feelings of a young person like this could well be the most important contribution one could make.

Vocational Choice Can Be Made Only by the Individual Himself

Good counseling always recognizes the integrity of the individual and respects his right and believes in his ability to make his own choice. Good vocational guidance does not consist in telling another person what he ought to do but in helping him understand himself and the world of work so that he can make a choice that is intelligent and meaningful to him. This is the only kind of choice that is mature and valid.

The counselor's task is not to provide the answers but to help the person find his own answers.

Vocational Choice Is a Process. It Requires Time

Vocational choice, like all other significant aspects of life, is a process—therefore, vocational guidance is a process. It is not an interview. One of the real dangers of a pastor as a vocational counselor is that he sees it as an interview. It is further complicated by the fact that those seeking guidance may see it as an interview. They came to the pastor, state their problem, and expect some advice that will provide a solution in an hour's time. This is not true only of the pastor, however. Much of the vocational guidance that is done in schools and elsewhere is what has been called "problem-point counseling" that is, it assists in making a decision in solving an immediate problem instead of guiding growth, understanding, and development.

Vocational choice is a complicated matter. The individual personality is complex, the world of work is complex. There is no way for two such complex factors to have a simple solution. This takes time. The counselor stands beside the person as a guide, not a dictator. He has the high privilege of sharing with a person as he works through one of the most important and far-reaching decisions in his life. In one sense he shares in his very destiny. This is a sacred responsibility.

Vocational Guidance Must Include One's Whole Philosophy of Life

Alfred North Whitehead, the famous philosopher, once said, "The common man needs to be convinced of the importance of the work he is doing." Unless one's vocation gives a man a sense of worth, a sense of personal responsibility, a sense of meaning, it is little more than a means of securing the food, clothing, and shelter that is necessary for life. A sense of value is sadly lacking in our culture. One investigation of the motivation behind men's vocational choice found that over 50% said it was to secure personal advancement, only 18% said it was the desire to render a service.[8]

Vocational guidance should include this wider perspective. It should create attitudes toward work that will dignify all forms of labor. It should help persons find the means not only of making a living but of rendering a service. It should help people find a sense of purpose in their work and thus in life itself.

[8] Cf. H. A. Greene, *Measurement of Human Behavior*, p. 558.

II

HISTORY OF VOCATONAL
GUIDANCE

Vocational guidance has been described as "the newest addition to the professions whose chief purpose is to help people with their problems."[1] This seems strange because the problem certainly isn't new. In the first century before Christ Cicero said, "We must decide what manner of men we wish to be and what calling in life we would follow; and this is the most difficult problem in the world."

Vocational guidance is one of those things that has had a long past but a short history. As a movement it is new. Most authorities date the beginning of the vocational guidance movement from the work of Frank Parsons and the date usually listed is 1908 when he founded the Vocation Bureau of Boston. It was in his first annual report that, as far as is known, the term "vocational guidance" first appeared in print.

In another sense vocational guidance is very old. As Cicero's statement indicates, men have been aware of vocational problems for centuries and young people discussed their questions of vocational choice with teachers, pastors, parents, and friends. As Brewer points out in his *History of Vocational Guidance*, "Long before vocational guidance was named,

[1] Sanderson, *op. cit.*, p. 3.

35

these devoted persons collected college catalogues, aroused ambition, studied aptitudes, counseled, paved the way ahead, and followed with friendly counsel over the years."[2] These people dealt not only with vocational problems but with all the problems of youth. There were others who were fore-runners, so to speak, of vocational guidance as such. As early as 1836 Edward Hazen published a textbook, *The Panorama of Professions and Trades*. In 1881, Lysander Richards proposed a new profession to help people find the right vocation. He called the profession "vocaphy," and the workers were to be known as "vocaphers." He envisioned a rather elaborate pro-gram by which the counselor would be able to evaluate the individual and know the requirements of all vocations and professions in order to place the individual in the one in which he would have the greatest success. He admitted that probably centuries would pass before his idea would be carried out. George A. Merrill came very close to establishing a vocational guidance program in his school in San Francisco in 1888, al-though it was actually a real experiment in vocational educa-cation with some individual vocational guidance.[3]

If we are going to understand vocational guidance today, we need to be familiar with some of the influences and trends that have changed it from a rather sporadic, occasional inci-dent to a definite movement and a speciality in its own right.

Frank Parsons and the Early Days of the Movement

Frank Parsons is rightfully considered the real founder of the vocational guidance movement. He was a teacher, lawyer, author, professor of law, and civic reformer. He became in-terested in the need for guidance early in his career. As early as 1894 he wrote,

[2] John M. Brewer, *History of Vocational Guidance* (New York: Harper & Brothers, 1942), p. 52. Used by permission.
[3] See *Ibid.*, pp. 124, 44, 49.

The training of a race-horse, and the care of sheep and chickens have been carried to the highest degree of perfection that intelligent planning can attain. But the education of a child, the choice of his employment are left very largely to the ancient haphazard plan—the struggle for existence, and the survival of the fittest.[4]

In 1905 he became director of the Breadwinners' Institute, a branch of the Civic Service House of Boston whose aim was to help young wage earners in both the cultural and practical aspects of life. Here in this social service agency he taught such courses as industrial history and economics, life principles, and gave vocational assistance to many men and women.

In 1907 he was asked to give a talk on the choice of a vocation to the senior class of one of the high schools in Boston. This speech was so well received that many of the young people requested a personal interview; this was the beginning of the individual counseling that was to lead to the plan of systematic vocational guidance.

In January, 1908, the Vocation Bureau of Boston was formed in the Civic Service House, with Parsons holding the title of Director and Vocational Counselor. On May 1, 1908, he made his first report to the executive committee. He advocated that vocational guidance

should become a part of the public school system in every community with experts trained as carefully in the art of vocational guidance as men are trained today for medicine and law, and supplied with every facility that science can devise for testing the senses and capacities and the whole physical, intellectual and emotional makeup of the child.[5]

Parson's book, Choosing a Vocation, which appeared in 1909, was the first book written from the point of view of the vocational guidance movement. The book was organized into three main areas: I. The Personal Investigation, II. The In-

[4] Ibid., p. 56.
[5] Ibid., Appendix B., p. 308.

dustrial Investigation, and III. The Organization and the Work. Many of Parson's principles and methods of counseling were quite modern in their viewpoint. In the report referred to above, he said,

No attempt is made of course to decide FOR the applicant what his calling should be; but the Bureau tries to help him arrive at a wise, well-founded conclusion for himself. . . . It helps the boy: 1st. To study and understand himself, his aptitudes, abilities, interests, resources and limitations and their causes; 2nd. To get a knowledge of the conditions of success, advantages and disadvantages, opportunities, etc., in different lines of industry; and 3rd. To reason correctly about the relations of these two groups of facts.[6]

There is little that would need to be changed in such a statement today.

The principles of counseling which Parsons outlined are still worthy of consideration:

1. It is better to choose a vocation than merely to "hunt a job."
2. No one should choose a vocation without careful self-analysis, thorough, honest, and under guidance.
3. The youth should have a large survey of the field of vocations, and not simply drop into the convenient or accidental position.
4. Expert advice, or the advice of men who have made a careful study of men and vocations and of the conditions of success, must be better and safer for a young man than the absence of it.
5. *Putting it down* on paper seems to be a simple matter, but is one of supreme importance.[7]

He was aware of the significance of aptitudes before any tests for their measurement were devised. He studied the needs of jobs and the trends of occupations. He created plans for the training of vocational counselors.

[6] *Ibid.*, Appendix B., p. 304.
[7] *Choosing a Vocation*, "Introductory Note."

Of course, there were others who worked with him, some of whom were of great assistiance, but Parsons himself was the motivating force behind the movement. Although he did not work in the public schools, he had the insight to see that vocational guidance should be a part of the public school program and he organized it in such a way that it could become part of the school program. He saw the need for and pioneered in the training of counselors. He utilized all the scientific techniques that were available and anticipated many others. As much as anything else he "recognized the significance of the work and enlisted others so that he guaranteed its continuance and expansion."[8]

Vocational Guidance and the Schools

While vocational guidance arose outside the schools, it was soon apparent that if it was to have any far-reaching value, it must become a part of the public school program. Parsons saw this; fortunately many school men saw it also. In some ways the relationship of the vocational guidance movement and education are similar to the relationship of the church school and the church. The church school movement arose outside the church, primarily as a philanthropy, but it was taken over by the church and became a permanent and valuable part of its program. So vocational guidance began in a social service agency and in its early years was conducted primarily by semi-public and philanthropic organizations, but educators recognized its value and it soon became a part of their concern.

Prior to 1900 the word "guidance" seldom appears in educational literature. Shortly after 1900 changing social conditions were such that educators almost of necessity had to face the need for guidance.

[8] Cf. Brewer, op. cit., p. 64.

The times were ripe for the emphasis that Parsons made. In fact, within a few years after he began his work, changing social conditions were such that vocational guidance became both natural and necessary. As great as was the need for vocational guidance in Parsons' day, within a few years the need was even greater. In fact, Parsons himself could scarcely have foreseen the almost phenomenal advances in science and the developments in technology and industry that would result. Comparatively speaking, prior to the twentieth century, it was relatively easy for parents, teachers, and friends to guide what high school and college graduates there were into the professions and business enterprises that were available to them.

Consider the situation of a student a generation or two ago. It was a rural and agricultural economy. Most people lived in small towns. A boy had relatively few choices. He either stayed on the farm, perhaps entered his father's business, or selected one of the professions. Contrast this with the multiplicity of choices confronted by a young person today. In the last quarter to half a century, science has created innumerable new types of jobs and specializations. Machine tool industries, the electrical industry, the automobile, airplane, radio, television, and refrigeration industries are but a few. Continued research and investigation have created specializations within such traditional professions as law, medicine, education, and the ministry. *The Dictionary of Occupational Titles*, published by the United States Employment Service, included descriptions of 17,452 different jobs in its first edition in 1939. In the second edition of 1949, there were 22,028 different jobs defined. The result is obvious. Choice of a life work had become so complicated that young people needed help. The schools recognized this need and tried to meet it.

At first vocational help in schools was limited to schools in larger communities. Superintendent Brooks, of the Boston schools, was one of the first to see the relationship between vocational education and vocational guidance. Primarily under the influence of Parsons a Committee on Vocational Advice was appointed by the Boston School Committee in 1909. In 1910 it reported that a vocational counselor had been appointed in each elementary and secondary school in Boston. Grand Rapids in 1912 was the first city to organize a department of vocational guidance although Cincinnati, Minneapolis, and Oakland were soon to follow. Before long other schools began to assume responsibility for some form of vocational guidance, but many of these early efforts were very inadequate. The teachers who were assigned the responsibility for some form of vocational counseling were often unprepared and untrained and usually added this service to a full teaching schedule. However, it was a beginning and the idea spread rapidly until, in a comparatively short time, some form of guidance was available in almost every school system.

It soon became obvious that vocational choice cannot be separated from educational planning. Changing conditions in the schools accentuated this problem and served both to stress the importance of guidance and to broaden its emphasis.

About the turn of the century, even as late as Parsons began his work, only about ten per cent of young people of high school age were enrolled in secondary schools. Within a few years, due to child labor laws, compulsory school laws, rising standards regarding education, and such factors, 70% to 90% were enrolled. In the school year 1947-48, for example, 81.6% of the school age population were in school.[9] This meant, not only larger numbers in school but a much wider range of interests and abilities. Arthur E. Traxler, speaking of this sudden increase in attendance, said that literally thousands of

[9] Cf. Crow & Crow, *Introduction to Guidance* (New York: American Book Co., 1951), p. 22.

young people were kept in school "who had no marked desire to be there, had no clear idea of why they were there or what they expected to get from their secondary school training, and did not know where they were going when they left school."[10]

Parallel with this rapid growth in attendance was an equally rapid expansion of curriculum. When Parsons began his work, a student had few problems as to educational planning because there was very little choice. The schools were forced to keep pace with the growing demand for practical and industrial education and also to expand their liberal and cultural offerings. The result was that the curriculum of colleges and secondary schools was expanded so rapidly and so broadly that a student was presented with a wide variety of choices and frequently with no background for making a choice and no guidance that would assist him. In a very brief time the curriculum of some schools not only doubled but tripled and in some cases increased as much as 100% to 300%. Because of such factors educators began to think in terms of educational guidance as well as vocational guidance. Truman Kelley is usually credited with being the first to use the term "educational guidance" in an official sense in a doctor's thesis of that title in 1915. He was thinking primarily of helping the student in a selection of high school subjects as an aid to vocational guidance.

Contributing Influences

At the same time that Parsons was carrying on his pioneer work and the schools were making their first experimental attempts at developing what were usually termed vocational guidance departments, other developments were taking place

[10] Traxler, *Techniques of Guidance* (New York: Harper & Brothers, 1945), p. 5. Used by permission.

that were to have a profound impact on vocational guidance in general and school guidance programs in particular. Two of the most important influences were the development of the mental testing movement and the developments in the field of psychology, particularly the special emphasis on the psychology of adolescence and the mental hygiene movement.

In 1905, the same year that Parsons began his Breadwinner's Institute in Boston, Alfred Binet in Paris published his first intelligence scale which was to form the basis for most mental testing. The year before G. Stanley Hall had published the first edition of his monumental *Adolescence* which was an important step in the child study movement. Parsons' book, *Choosing a Vocation*, was published posthumously in 1909. In 1908 Clifford Beers published *A Mind that Found Itself* which was really the initial impetus in the development of the mental hygiene movement. It is noteworthy that all of these concepts were evolved independently of each other.

The mental measurement movement soon became an accepted part of American education. No man was more influential in this field than Edward L. Thorndike whose famous statement, "Whatever exists at all, exists in some amount and therefore can be measured" became a byword. The mental measurement movement made people aware of the reality and the significance of individual differences in abilities, interests, and capacities. This was profoundly important for vocational guidance. The development of objective tests had an influence beyond the actual tests themselves. They made clear beyond question the fact that there are large differences among individuals in terms of ability, interest, aptitude, and temperament and thus great variation in their potentialities for success or failure both academically and vocationally.

At the same time it made available instruments which could measure qualities of intelligence and achievement and aptitude. All of this came at the time that the recognized need for guidance gave the guidance movement techniques with which they could work. In fact, the influence of the measurement movement has been so great that some guidance departments conceived of their task primarily as the giving of tests, often without considering how they would use them, and sometimes to the neglect of counseling.

The mental hygiene movement, the developments in such fields as psychoanalysis, depth psychology, child and adolescent psychology did not emphasize techniques as much as a general philosophy and point of view. The mental hygiene movement directed attention to the importance of the emotional life of the child, the significance of family relationships, the reality of unconscious motivation, the importance of "feelings" as well as abilities and aptitudes.

It became apparent in actual experience that a young person's educational problem may be the result of an emotional or family problem and his vocational difficulty may be due to feelings of inadequacy or poor interpersonal relationships.

The result was a shift in emphasis from vocational and educational guidance to guidance of the "whole" child, as the "whole" person. The vocational aspect was still strong but vocational guidance was seen in relationship to all other factors. Schools which had originally listed vocational guidance departments changed them to guidance departments or personnel services.

This has been treated very briefly but it has had a profound influence on education in general. Arthur J. Jones, professor in the School of Education of the University of Pennsylvania said, "One of the most significant developments in education during the past quarter century is the guidance movement."[11] James

---

[11] Jones: *Principles of Guidance* (New York: McGraw-Hill Book Company, Inc., 1945), p. ix. Used by permission.

B. Conant while he was still president of Harvard wrote, ". . . it would not be too much to say that the success or failure of our guidance program hangs in all probability on the success or failure of our system of public education."[12]

Other Agencies

The schools were not the only ones interested or active in vocational guidance. The vocational guidance movement began in a social service agency and in its early years was conducted as such. Private bureaus, similar to the one established by Parsons in Boston, were created in other cities. Many early programs of vocational guidance were conducted by social service agencies like the Henry Street Settlement in New York which had a Vocational Guidance Committee to help the young people of the underprivileged district.

Parsons had originally worked closely with the Y.M.C.A. in Boston; in fact, he mentions the co-operation of this organization in his first report. Other Y's became interested in the subject and adopted Parsons' idea. Some of the programs were well conceived and directed. Some Y's yet have guidance departments and full-time secretaries for guidance work. The Y.W.C.A. in some localities also has been active in vocational guidance and in placement as well.

In 1910 the National Urban League was established "to further the industrial advancement of the Negro." It included vocational guidance for Negroes as a part of its program. The B'nai B'rith Hillel Foundation carries on extensive vocational guidance for Jewish Youth.

The organization of the Employment Managers' Association in 1912 marked an awareness of a new profession, the

[12] In Rothney and Roens, *Guidance of American Youth* (Cambridge: Harvard University Press, 1950), p. xi.

personnel worker in industry. In 1925 the National Rehabilitation Association was established to promote vocational guidance of the handicapped.

The Federal Government entered the field of vocational guidance with the establishment of the Occupational Information and Guidance Service in the Vocational Division of the United States Office of Education (1938) and in the establishment of the United States Employment Service. This resulted in the establishment of employment centers throughout the country as well as in increased research and in many significant publications, most notable of which was the Dictionary of Occupational Titles in 1939.

Vocational Guidance as a Movement

In less than 50 years after Parsons conceived his idea, vocational guidance has acquired what can rightfully be called a movement. When Parsons started the Breadwinner Institute, he was the only full-time vocational guidance worker. At present there are thousands of vocational counselors. Some are working in school systems, some on counseling staffs of universities, some with private agencies, some in government and industry. Now vocational counseling can be listed as a separate profession or specialty.

The vocational guidance movement has developed an *organization* that is national in scope. The first conference on vocational guidance on a national scale was held in Boston in 1910. By 1913 there was sufficient interest and participation to form a National Vocational Guidance Association. For several years its membership was small, and attendance at its meetings limited, but it has grown to include many branches and a total membership that numbers several thousand.

The vocational guidance movement has developed its own

literature. A *Vocational Guidance News-Letter* was first published in 1911; it later became the *Vocational Guidance Bulletin* and then was further expanded into the *Vocational Guidance Magazine.* In 1933 it took the title *Occupations,* under which it had a very wide influence. In 1952 the name was again changed, this time including a little broader scope and being called *The Personnel and Guidance Journal.*

Since Frank Parsons published his *Choosing a Vocation* in 1909, a steady stream of books has appeared on vocational guidance as such, and it has been a major emphasis in almost all books on "guidance" in general.

The bibliography of Donald Super's *Psychology of Careers,* published in 1957, listed 382 different references to books and articles, which gives some indication of the extent of the publications that have appeared.

Vocational guidance has developed its own special *training* both at the undergraduate and the graduate levels. Prior to the time of Parsons what vocational guidance there was was of an informal nature. The first school to offer a course for the training of vocational counselors was Harvard, in the summer of 1911. Other schools soon followed Harvard's example. A survey of schools in 1948 showed that more than 70 were offering such courses and by 1941 the number had increased to more than 260. Now it is an accepted part of most teachers' colleges, colleges, and universities.

Primarily through the efforts of such schools the vocational guidance movement has continued to refine and improve its techniques. Parsons saw the need for better techniques but had very few to draw upon. The vocational guidance movement was strongly influenced by the testing movement. When the educational psychologists developed tests of intelligence and educational achievement, their relationship to vocational guidance was obvious. Those interested primarily in vocational problems developed tests of vocational interest and aptitude. These will be discussed again in a later chapter.

Much effort and research went into the development of such instruments. Dr. Strong at Stanford spent nineteen years of investigation in the development of the Strong Vocational Interest Inventory, which appeared in 1927. Brewer characterizes this as "among the most important contributions of the vocational guidance movement." In 1939 Frederick Kuder published his Vocational Preference Record which has been widely used. Other tests were developed and are continuing to be developed.

As guidance became an accepted part of education and as school populations increased, it was recognized that no individual could remember all the information needed about any one person. Rather, teachers, counselors, psychologists, and all who dealt with the child needed to pool their information to provide a total picture. The *cumulative record* was the result. A great deal of study, experimentation, and research has gone into the development of adequate records. These include not only objective test scores, but academic records, health records, extracurricular activities, family history, anecdotal records, rating scales—in fact, any information that is related to a young person and his experience.

Means and techniques of discovering and disseminating occupational information were created. The interview itself came under scrutiny and evaluation. In fact, two distinct schools of thought developed over the approach that should be taken in counseling. One school, under the leadership of E. G. Williamson, advocated what is called a clinical or directive approach, while another group, under the leadership of Carl Rogers, advocated what was at first called a non-directive, but was later changed to a "client-centered" approach. This controversy has had a profound influence on vocational guidance as a whole.

It has forced many to rethink their whole philosophy of guidance and to revise some of their basic assumptions and to alter or change their methods of approach. We shall return to this matter of counseling when we discuss the principles and techniques of vocational guidance in later chapters.

In a comparatively brief time since its origin those working in the vocational guidance movement have done considerable research. This has included historical research such as that of Dr. Brewer. It has included research into various techniques, into job satisfaction and motivation, into the relationship of intelligence, interest, aptitude, personality to vocational success. However, it is still in its early stages.

Changing Emphases in Vocational Guidance

In a comparatively brief period of time (less than fifty years) the vocational guidance movement not only grew in numbers of participants and in the development of methods and techniques, but it also showed a marked change in emphasis and point of view.

From an occasional sporadic effort on the part of a few interested individuals it has grown to an organized and effective movement. From a friendly concerned desire to help it has grown to a profession, trained and prepared to use specialized skills and techniques. From one man's idea in a social service agency it has become an accepted part of all schools and colleges in the country; it is included in many social service agencies and is utilized extensively by government and industry.

In the early days of the movement the primary concern was to help a person select a vocation and find a job. At this time this was the most apparent need. Gradually there came the realization that vocational choice could not be separated from other aspects of life and the emphasis was on "guidance"—not just vocational guidance. This does not mean that vocational choice has been minimized or overlooked. It means vocational guidance is now seen as a part of, and a very important part of, the total guidance of the individual; it no longer is the only emphasis, but it is a part of a total or larger emphasis.

Perhaps the most noteworthy change in emphasis was from the giving of advice about vocational choice to helping an individual make his own vocational choice. It was a change from doing something to or for an individual to doing something with an individual. There has been a decided shift from a more or less authoritarian paternal approach to a more permissive mental hygiene approach. This can be seen quite graphically in the definitions that have been given to vocational guidance as such.

In 1924 the definition adopted by the National Vocational Guidance Association read, "Vocational Guidance is the giving of information, experience, and advice in regard to choosing an occupation, preparing for it, entering it, and progressing in it." When the definition was revised in 1937, instead of saying the "giving of advice" vocational guidance was described as the "process of assisting the individual to choose an occupation, to prepare himself for entrance into it, to enter it and make progress in it."

The Church and the Vocational Guidance Movement

It is quite obvious that in the discussion of the history of vocational guidance the church has been conspicuous by its absence. This does not mean the church or the ministry did nothing. Individual pastors on occasion discussed vocational plans with young people. This was especially true of those who were considering the ministry. The vocational guidance that was done prior to Parsons' time was done by teachers and professors; in the early days of higher education in this country many of these were clergymen. E. G. Williamson, speaking of the early American universities, says, "During this period, faculties were composed largely of soul-centered clergymen, enrollments were small, and professors were more interested in teaching individual students than in prosecuting research."[13] He continues to emphasize the value of this informal friendly type of guidance, although in no wise contends that it is vocational guidance as we think of it today.

As far as the contemporary vocational guidance movement is concerned, we have not mentioned the church because it has had very little to say. Not that there has been any opposition; the church has largely been unaware of its relationship.

At the same time the vocational guidance movement was developing, the religious education movement and the pastoral counseling movement were developing within the church. Neither has made an attempt to relate the findings of vocational guidance to the work of the religious educator or the pastoral counselor. In fact, one can go through the major publications of either religious education or pastoral counseling and he will only find an occasional reference to vocational guidance.

A study of the table of contents of several standard volumes on pastoral counseling reveals chapters on the sick, the sorrowing, the shut-in, the aged, the alcoholic, marriage conflict, premarital problems, etc., etc., but no chapter on vocational guidance.

That the pastor and the church need to understand vocational guidance, and that they have something unique and vital to contribute to vocational guidance is the thesis and major purpose of the rest of this study.

[13] Williamson, *How to Counsel Students* (New York: McGraw-Hill Book Company, Inc., 1939). Used by permission.

III

BASIC TECHNIQUES
OF VOCATIONAL GUIDANCE:
THE INTERVIEW AND
PSYCHOLOGICAL TESTS

Good vocational guidance depends primarily upon two things: (1) understanding the individual, and (2) understanding the world of work. One cannot do effective vocational counseling with a person unless he understands that person, his abilities and aptitudes, his strengths and limitations, his likes and dislikes, his hopes and ambitions, his feelings and attitudes. Nor can one do effective vocational guidance unless he understands the world of work, that is, what various occupations require in the way of training and ability and what the nature of these occupations really is.

Good vocational choice depends upon the same two things: (1) understanding oneself and (2) understanding the world of work.

An individual must be aware of his own possibilities and limitations, his own likes and dislikes; he must know what he wants to do and where he is most likely to find success and satisfaction. In order to do this he also must know the world of work. He must know what possibilities are available for him and how to evaluate one against the other. He can not make an intelligent and realistic choice of a specific vocation unless he knows what that choice involves. He can not make a choice of one vocation unless he can compare its advantages and disadvantages with those of other vocations.

The vocational counselor's task is to help the individual get such a realistic understanding of himself and of the vocational possibilities that he can make a decision that is intelligent, realistic, and his own.

In order to do these two things certain techniques have been developed.

THE COUNSELING INTERVIEW

The interview is the basic technique in vocational counseling as in all other areas of counseling. Vocational guidance has developed its own specialized techniques such as vocational and psychological tests and occupational information services. These will be discussed at length because they are not well known, especially by religious workers.

These techniques are dependent on the interview because it is through the counseling interview that test results are interpreted and occupational information is made available and meaningful.

Nothing can take the place of a face-to-face, one-to-one relationship. The interview has been defined as a conversation with a purpose. It is a conversation in which one person with a problem comes to another who is qualified to help. The interview has many purposes and objectives.

It is through the interview that a friendly, confident relationship is established. This relationship determines the degree of rapport between the counselor and counselee on which all effective counseling depends. It is through the interview (along with other methods) that the counselor gains some understanding of the counselee. It is through the interview that the counselor imparts to the student information that is necessary for educational and vocational choices and decisions.

It is through the interview that the student drains off emotion, releases tension, reduces anxiety so that he can think clearly and plan wisely. It is thus through the interview that the student gains an understanding of himself, his own feelings, his strengths and weaknesses, his past experiences and future possibilities.

It is through the interview that goals are clarified, and guidance is given in the making of plans and taking steps of definite action.

There is much difference of opinion as to how all this is best accomplished. There are some who would say this "conversation with a purpose" should be directed primarily by the counselor. This would be the traditional approach in vocational counseling. Here the counselor on the basis of the data available would suggest courses of action and give definite advice. Others of the client-centered point of view contend that the counselee should be the center of focus, the counselor's responsibility is to reflect feeling and clarify statements.

We shall not review the controversy between the directive or clinical school of thought as against the more permissive or client-centered approach. This has been done too frequently to need repetition here. We would point out that anyone who would accept responsibility in this field must be familiar with both points of view.

One cannot even read the literature without understanding the principles involved. It makes considerable difference whether one is reading a book by Carl Rogers or one of his followers or by E. G. Williamson or one of his colleagues. The approach to the counseling interview are quite different.

There is a strong trend, especially in the vocational guidance field, to utilize the values of both approaches. In the early days the vocational guidance movement was strongly directive. This was quite natural and was true of all counseling at that time. The impact of what was originally called the non-directive, and later came to be known as client-centered, school of thought on the vocational guidance movement has been very strong.

It is now recognized that many vocational problems are highly involved emotionally and where much emotion is present, it is well to be permissive or nondirective. Only as these feelings are accepted and understood can best results be achieved. Many feel that it is best to be more permissive in the early stages of counseling in order that emotions can be drained off and a good relationship established and in order that the counselor will be sure he is dealing with the main issue. With the retarded, or those of limited ability, it is sometimes necessary to be directive. They cannot come to insights as effectively and are likely to make unrealistic choices and thus need more guidance and direction. When problems of vocational choice or adjustment are complicated by other factors, such as family disagreement, feelings of inadequacy, and so forth, it is well to be more permissive.

In actual practice most counselors use both directive and nondirective approaches, sometimes with the same person, or within the same interview, depending on the person and the nature of the problem. Many nondirective counselors are more directive than they realize, most directive counselors recognize that the client, as they call him, must ventilate his feelings and make his own decisions. The wise vocational counselor will be thoroughly versed in each method and use the one that is most effective in each individual case.

MENTAL AND VOCATIONAL TESTS

The vocational guidance movement has been deeply indebted to the mental measurement movement. In fact, mental and vocational tests are one of the primary techniques for understanding the individual and helping him understand himself. Mental testing is a complex field in itself. Certain areas are specifically related to the field of vocational guidance.

Mental Ability Tests

The most common psychological tests are the tests of mental ability sometimes referred to as intelligence tests or IQ tests. The latter term is not a good description because not all tests give an IQ score. Several give their results in terms of a percentile rank which many authorities prefer. Perhaps the term "scholastic aptitude" test is as accurate a description as any because, as much as anything else, these tests measure the ability to do academic work.

Mental ability tests may be divided into four types:

(1) *Individual tests,* such as the Stanford-Binet and the Wechsler-Bellevue Scale, are administered to one individual at a time by a trained psychometrist. These are the most accurate and obviously the most time-consuming and expensive.

(2) *Group tests* are mainly paper-and-pencil tests that can be administered to a whole group of people at once. They are not as accurate as the individual tests, but they do enable the counselor to get a fairly reliable measure on a whole class or group at one sitting. Among the more common group tests are the Otis Quick-Scoring Test of Mental Ability, the Henmon-Nelson test of Mental Ability, the California Mental Maturity Tests, the Ohio State University Psychological Examination, and many others.

(3) *Performance tests* were created in order to secure an evaluation of those who had a language problem, such as the foreign born and people from underprivileged areas who had not had the opportunity for schooling.

(4) *Special tests* are designed for use with special problem areas such as the deaf, the blind, spastic children, or one who would be at a disadvantage if attempting to take one of the other tests.

Since different occupations require different levels of intelligence, the place of tests of mental ability in vocational guidance is obvious. They may be more accurate in predicting failure than in predicting success. If a person lacks the mental ability to perform a vocational task, then the possibilities for success in that task are simply not present. However, many other factors must be present in order to guarantee success. Sufficient level of intelligence says only that the person has the mental ability; he must also have the desire, the interest, the perseverance, the personality and all other things that go with vocational success.

Actually, as Dr. McKinney points out, an intelligence test indicates whether or not a person has the ability to secure the education and training for a position more accurately than it predicts whether or not he will enjoy or succeed in this field.[1] This, however, is extremely important; so important, in fact, that we would almost say it is the place to begin in making vocational plans.

Tests of Educational Skill and Achievement

A second area of testing, used most commonly by the schools, is that known as educational achievement tests. We

[1] Cf. Fred McKinney, *Counseling for Personal Adjustment* (New York: Houghton Mifflin Co., 1958), p. 403.

are speaking here of tests standardized on national norms, not of teacher-made tests to determine the grade or achievement of a particular class.

It is commonly recognized that teachers' grades are quite subjective and variable. The research of educational psychologists has made this quite clear. One hundred English teachers were asked to grade a composition, assign to it a percentage value, and indicate the school grade in which they would expect that quality of work to be done. The percentage grades ranged from 60 to 98, and the estimated grade location varied from fifth to the junior level in college. In a similar study, 116 high school teachers were asked to grade the same geometry paper, and the values ranged from 28 to 92.[2] It was even found that college instructors assigned different marks when they regraded their own papers, after a period of time, without a knowledge of the former mark they had given.

These illustrations are not given to destroy faith in teachers' grades but simply to point up a fact which every teacher and educational psychologist knows—grades are very subjective in nature. However, they are of real value in estimating what a person can do.

To meet this problem the objective, standardized test of educational achievement was developed. The mental ability test was created to determine how much mental ability a student had. The educational achievement test was developed to determine how much use he had made of that ability. In other words, the purpose of the achievement test is to determine in as accurate and objective a way as possible how much a person has learned from the educational experience. Some tests measure achievement in a single subject such as English or social studies, others cover several areas of learning.

[2] Cf. C. C. Ross, *Measurement in Today's Schools* (New York: Prentice Hall, Inc., 1947), p. 45.

Achievement tests have a value in vocational counseling in pointing out the areas in which a person has gained some degree of mastery. A young man considering the ministry, for example, should have a fairly good score on an achievement test in English or he would have cause for some concern.

Achievement tests are also good indications of the amount of training one could reasonably expect to secure. Some feel that achievement tests are as good prediction of success in college as are intelligence tests. The best results are obtained when both ability tests and achievement tests are used in conjunction with each other.

A word should be said about reading tests. These tests are designed to measure a person's reading rate and comprehension. Perhaps no skill is as important for advanced academic work as the ability to read rapidly and with understanding. Anyone who is considering one of the professions that requires advanced education should score well on an achievement test in reading. Fortunately, this is something that can often be corrected if a weakness is detected soon enough. This is one of the major values of such a test.

Vocational Interest Tests

Two types of tests developed primarily for the vocational guidance movement were vocational interest tests and vocational aptitude tests. The simplest definiion of an interest is simply something that a person likes to do. In terms of vocational choice, a person will do better, will persist longer, will find greater satisfaction if he finds a job in which he is genuinely interested. As one text puts it, "Interest is the driving power leading to success."[3]

[3] Walter James Greenleaf, *Occupations and Careers* (New York: McGraw-Hill Book Company, 1955), p. 18.

The question is, how can you tell what a person's interests are? The simplest answer is, "Ask him." In some cases this is enough. But actually it is not as easy as that. Many young people do not know what they are interested in—especially as it relates to vocational choice. Young people have such limited and often erroneous knowledge of and experience in jobs that it is difficult for them to say whether their interests are in line with what a person does in a vocation. There are many subtle factors that influence a person at this point. Many a girl has said she was interested in nursing when actually she was interested in interns. Many people have expressed interests in law, medicine, the ministry, or some other of the professions which really turn out to be an admiration of someone in the profession. Or they are interested in the prestige and glamor sometimes associated with the profession instead of in the actual work that one in the profession is called upon to do. To meet such problems as these, interest tests were devised.

The measurement of interest was not begun until about the twenties but since then has expanded very rapidly. It has been the subject of much investigation and research. In fact vocational interest is one of the most thoroughly investigated areas of all mental measurements.

Two of the most widely used interest tests are the Strong Vocational Interest Blank and the Kuder Preference Record.

Strong's test appeared in 1927. A few quotations from his book *The Vocational Interests of Men and Women*, which gives the results of his research and instructions for the use of his test, give his point of view.

Men engaged in occupations . . . have a characteristic pattern of likes and dislikes which differentiate them from men in other occupations.

. . . .

It is assumed that, if a man likes to do the things which men like who are successful in a given occupation and dislikes to do the things which these same men dislike to do, he will feel at home in that occupational environment. Seemingly, also, he should be more effective there than somewhere else, because he will be engaged, in the main, in work he likes.[4]

The inventory was designed to provide a means whereby a person's interests thus could be compared to those who had been successful in the specific occupations.

The Kuder Preference Record, on the other hand, measures preferences for different kinds of personal and social activities. His instrument compares the student's interest to those of the general population in such areas as outdoor activity, mechanical, computational, scientific, persuasive, artistic, literary, musical, social service, and clerical. Kuder has recently published another test which measures interest in terms of specific vocations. There have been several other tests devised all of which are created for the same purpose to gain a reasonably accurate and objective measure of a person's interests as related to vocational activity.

As a result of the research and clinical experience with vocational interest inventories, certain conclusions and principles have been agreed upon that should guide anyone who is working in the vocational guidance field.

First of all, it should be pointed out that a measure of vocational interest is not a measure of vocational ability or aptitude. There is often confusion at this point. Often times a young person or his parent will be heard to say the tests show he is qualified for a science or art or some other field, when all he has taken is an interest inventory. This may or may not be true. Interest measures and measures of aptitude and

---

[4] Edward K. Strong, Jr., *Vocational Interests of Men and Women*, (Stanford: Stanford University Press, 1943), pp. 47, 56. Used by permission.

ability are two quite distinct areas of measurement. Interest tests have to do with a person's attitudes and feeling towards a vocation; they say much about the direction of his efforts and the satisfaction he will receive from it. They say nothing about the level of his achievement. Good vocational guidance takes both into account—what he can do and what he will want to do.

Interest inventories are not valid until middle or later adolescence. Most of the experts feel that interest patterns remain fairly constant after about eighteen years of age. There are exceptions, but in the main, research shows that a man's interests at twenty will be pretty much his interests at forty. Interest tests given during adolescence are useful guides but it must be recognized they are subject to change; after the teens they change little.

It is recognized that interest inventories can be faked; that is, a class can be instructed to respond like engineers and in the main they can be quite successful in making themselves look like engineers in terms of their interests. This does not limit the usefulness of inventories in counseling. It is assumed that such an atmosphere can be created and such instructions given that the individual will make a sincere response. When this is done, an interest measure can be very helpful.

Interest tests are seen as a very useful source of data about a person, not the only source. No one knows exactly how close one's interests need to be to others' in a vocation in order to attain satisfaction and success in the vocation. There are wide variations of interest within any one field, such as engineering for example. Therefore, they should be interpreted carefully and cautiously and, used in this manner, have been found very helpful by vocational counselors and guidance workers.

Vocational Aptitude Tests

The other area of testing developed primarily for the vocational guidance movement is the vocational aptitude test. An aptitude is defined as "the ability or collection of abilities, required to perform a specified practical activity." The essential characteristic of an aptitude is that it already exists before training and therefore can be measured. In other words, an aptitude test determines whether or not a person will benefit from training. An aptitude test measures a potentiality. Training takes the potentiality and converts it into a skill.

The purpose of the aptitude test is to help predict how rapidly and well a person is likely to benefit from the training. It has been pointed out that an aptitude test is more likely to predict failure than it is success. If a person lacks the potential, the possibilities for success are very small. If a person has an aptitude, he is not guaranteed success unless he also has the interest, the persistence, the ability to get along with others, and all the other factors that make for success.

Aptitude tests are based on several assumptions that are now so well established by research they are quite generally accepted:

(1) There are a number of special aptitudes such as musical aptitude, mechanical aptitude, etc., which can be measured.

(2) Individuals differ in the extent to which they possess any given aptitude. Some are well endowed in certain areas, others have very limited abilities.

(3) These aptitudes remain relatively stable, that is, they tend to persist so that what is measured today can reasonably be expected to be present tomorrow.

America has assumed the leadership in aptitude tests. The Seashore Measures of Musical Talent appeared in 1919. In 1918 the Stenquist Mechanical Ability Test was presented. Since then the field has expanded very rapidly. Besides musical and mechanical abilities tests were developed in art, clerical ability, stenography, typing, teaching, nursing, engineering, selling, and a variety of other fields. A word of caution should be included here. Most aptitude tests are more accurate in predicting success in beginning courses than they are in predicting success at the professional level. Now aptitude tests are usually given in batteries. The United States Employment Service, for example, gives a General Aptitude Test Battery that gives results in ten areas: (1) general intelligence, (2) verbal aptitude, (3) numerical aptitude, (4) spatial aptitude, (5) form perception, (6) clerical perception, (7) eye-hand co-ordination, (8) motor speed, (9) finger dexterity and (10) manual dexterity. These aptitudes are then related to the needs of twenty occupational fields—over 2,000 occupations.

The value of a knowledge of one's aptitudes in vocational choice is obvious, but Walter Bingham, a specialist in aptitude testing, issues a pertinent warning when he says, "to gain a clear understanding of one's aptitudes is an achievement of years rather than hours."[5]

Personality Tests

Another area of testing that has had a wide popularity is in the so-called tests of character and personality. Over five hundred such tests have appeared in recent years. These tests consist of paper and pencil tests where the subject responds to certain statements and questions that are designed to indicate emotional stability and maturity, word association tests, sentence completion tests, and the more complicated projective techniques such as the Rorschach ink blot test or the Thematic

[5] Bingham: *Aptitudes and Aptitude Testing*, (New York: Harper and Brothers, 1937), p. 12.

Apperception Test in which the individual tells a story of his own creation about a series of ambiguous pictures which reveals his own personality pattern.

These tests have not been widely used in vocational counseling and rightfully so. At the present time there is very little data on the relationship of personality test scores to vocational success or satisfaction. Such tests are much more difficult to administer and interpret and should be used only by those trained and qualified to use them. When misused they can do much harm.

Personality tests should be used in vocational counseling only when the counselor is also a trained psychologist and even then only when there is a question about the person's emotional stability that would have a bearing on his vocational choice and adjustment.

When these tests are used with such precautions they can be very helpful, as in the selection of missionary candidates, for example.

PRINCIPLES OF VOCATIONAL TESTING

Psychological testing in vocational guidance is now so well established that certain general principles are recognized that should govern such procedures.

Dangers of Testing

As in all procedures there are dangers that need to be recognized and avoided. One danger is that people will be too enthusiastic, place too much confidence in tests; the other is that people will not be enthusiastic enough and do not recognize the values they possess. Some people see tests as a cure-all, an answer to all their problems. The specialists in testing warn against such superficial enthusiasm. Jane Warters reminds us tests are not fortunetelling devices that have a simple and easy answer to all one's problems.

Another danger is that the use of tests, which appear to be very objective and precise, may lead to the neglect of other procedures such as counseling, observation, and all the other methods which also give an insight into human behavior.

The fact that so many tests are available can create another danger. Not all tests are equally valid. In fact many are inferior and not proven experimentally. To accept tests without critical examination and a thorough check on their validity is to be untrue to the basic principles of testing.

Another danger is not to use them at all. This is the danger that persons, such as a minister or director of religious education, YMCA worker, someone who is called upon to do occasional vocational counseling is most likely to yield to. In discounting their value, or in merely neglecting to go to the trouble to get test results, he faces the greater problem of attempting to make an evaluation based only on his own observation and opinion—which in many cases is little more than a guess.

The Values of Testing

Testing has certain dangers that need to be avoided, yet it also has values that need to be recognized. Tests do provide information that can be secured in no other way. This information is objective and standardized. It frees a person from the necessity of guessing about abilities, of relying on his own observation, his own opinion.

It provides information in meaningful terms. Test information enables the counselor to evaluate each student in relation to all students, or in relation to a particular group of students with whom he is or will be competing. Norm groups have been developed on high school students, college freshmen, college graduates, people in certain professions or areas of work, for example, so that it is possible to compare the abilities and aptitudes of an individual student with those of a particular group. Because of this it is possible to make reasonable predictions as to possible success in college or some other training program.

Testing can save a great deal of time. It is possible to come to a reasonable degree of accuracy as to a person's abilities by watching him in various situations over a long period of time. Through a battery of tests a reasonably accurate evaluation of his abilities can be made in one afternoon. Furthermore, by such methods information about a class of fifty can be secured as readily as about one.

One of the primary values of testing is that it saves the counselor from making mistakes. It provides a check on all other methods such as counseling, observation, grades, the opinions of others, and so forth.

Principles of Testing

In order to avoid the dangers and utilize the values certain principles should govern the use of tests.

(1) *Tests should be selected with great care.*

——It must be recognized that there are poor tests on the market. Only the best tests should be used.

——In working with any individual (or group for that matter), tests should be selected to fit the individual and meet his needs.

——In individual counseling it is a good idea for the individual to have an active part in the selection of the tests. This helps him understand the nature of testing and prepares him for the interpretation of testing.

(2) *Tests should be administered and interpreted only by those qualified and trained to do so.*

——Testing is a specialized skill and when misused can do harm. Florence Goodenough reminds us that tests are not like the telephone that anyone can pick up and use.

——It is felt by some that it is better if the same person does not give the tests and do the counseling. It is difficult to go through the necessary procedures required in testing and be reflective and permissive in counseling with the same person.

(3) *Tests should be used only for the purpose for which they were intended.*

——It should be recognized that each test was constructed for a definite and specific purpose. A test of mental abilities does not say anything about motivation for example. A high score on a mental ability test says a person could succeed in college; it doesn't say he will.

——A test of vocational interest is not a test of vocational aptitude. High scientific interest may or may not mean a boy will be a successful scientist.

(4) *All tests should be used with caution.*

——All methods of evaluation have their limitations. We must recognize that tests can be wrong. When there is doubt, retesting is in order. Improper wording of the instructions, a handicap in reading, poor motivation—any one of a number of things may have prevented getting an accurate measure.

——A low test should be rechecked for reasons mentioned above; it may not be the true picture.

——A decision should never be made on the basis of one

test alone. By this we mean any decision that affects a person's future career and his future well-being should be made only with thorough and accurate information.

(5) *Tests should be used in conjunction with all other means of evaluation.*

——The human personality is so complex, the problem of vocational choice and adjustment is so complicated that no decision should be made on the basis of test information alone.

——Test information should be combined with the interview, observation, evaluation of others, any method that helps to give a thorough and complete picture of the individual.

(6) *It should be recognized that there are some aspects of personality that no tests can measure.*

——Mental tests can measure some areas, such as mental abilities and vocational aptitudes, with a fair degree of accuracy, yet there are other areas such as persistence, imagination, motivation that can scarcely be measured at all.

——Vocational success depends not only upon aptitudes and ability but also on social skills, the ability to get along with one's workers. These are areas that are far more difficult to measure, and some of them cannot be measured at all.

(7) *All testing must be thorough.*

——It is unethical and unfair to make permanent decisions on one or two tests when more thorough and complete testing would give a more accurate and complete picture.

(8) *A person's attitude toward tests and test results can strongly influence the value he derives from the testing.*

——The nature and purpose of testing should be interpreted to the person in order that the counselor can gain his co-operation and understanding.

——The use the counselee makes of test information will depend upon his understanding of the meaning of the information and his attitudes toward the information.

(9) *Information about test results should be given only in the form of general interpretation and only to the degree that a person can understand and accept it.*

——Because there is often misunderstanding as to the meaning of exact scores results of testing should be given in the form of general interpretation that will make their meaning clear to the individual.

The counselor has the moral obligation of making the individual aware of both his limitations and his possibilities as they are revealed in test findings. Such information should usually be related to other information regarding educational achievement, vocational possibilities, future plans, and so forth.

Test information should be handled in such a way that a person can accept it emotionally and apply it to his own life.

(10) *Test interpretation should be done as a part of the general counseling process.*

——Test results should be presented in such a manner that the individual has ample opportunity to express his own feelings and concerns and that the counselor can utilize such methods as reflection and clarification.

——At times it may be advisable to give test results over a period of time, perhaps in several interviews.

——When test results necessitate the changing of vocational plans or the altering of a person's concept of himself, ample time should be provided for the expression of feelings and a continuing counseling process.

——Giving test results is a part of a counseling process and the counselor, here as in all counseling, follows the counselee's leads and lets him take the iniative if he wishes.

IV

BASIC TECHNIQUES
OF VOCATIONAL GUIDANCE:
OCCUPATIONAL INFORMATION
AND REFERRAL

The first sentence of Carroll Leonard Shartle's book entitled *Occupational Information* says, "Millions of decisions are made each day on the basis of occupational information."

Good vocational guidance depends upon understanding the world of work. Good vocational choice depends upon an individual understanding himself and also understanding the job he is considering, its qualifications and requirements, its true nature, its comparison with other jobs. Only as a person has understanding in both areas can he make an intelligent and mature choice.

The fact is that many young people make vocational choices with meager or inadequate knowledge about vocations and not infrequently with misinformation. It is almost safe to say that when a young person seeks vocational guidance it is only rarely that he possesses accurate or complete information. In fact, the opposite is more often the case. As Raymond G. Kuhlen points out in his *Psychology of Adolescent Development*,

73

many young people make vocational choices against a background of "misinformation, inconsistency, and fantasy."

In one sense this is not surprising. The world of work is so vast and complex, it is almost impossible for the counselor to accumulate and organize accurate information when he is trained to do so and makes a special effort to do so, let alone the student with his limited experience and background. It is particularly true of some occupations which are not of the nature that can be observed by the general public. It is further complicated by the fact that many people's opinions about some vocations are secured from movies and TV, books and magazines, and may be more misleading than accurate, for the picture is romanticized or presents a one-sided view of the nature of the occupation.

A vocational decision that is made on the basis of information that is inaccurate or incomplete can lead to many unfortunate mistakes. For this reason it is important that both counselor and counselee have adequate information on which an intelligent choice can be made.

To meet this need the vocational guidance movement has developed techniques for securing accurate and usable information about occupations, families of occupations, occupational trends, and anything that pertains to an understanding of the world of work.

Like almost everything else in this study, this is not something entirely new. For centuries men have been giving information about occupations and vocations. A book bearing the title *The Book of Trends or Library of the Useful Arts* appeared as early as 1807. It consisted of three volumes, each one describing twenty or more trades. In 1837 a book appeared with the interesting title:

The COMPLETE book of Trades; or Parents' Guide and Youth's Instructor forming a popular Encyclopedia of Trades, Manu-

factures, and Commerce, as at present pursued in England; with a More Particular Regard to its state in and Near the Metropolis; including a Copious Table of Every Trade, Profession, Occupation, and Calling, However divided and subdivided; together with the Apprentice Fee usually given with Each, and an Estimate of the Sums required for Commencing Business.

Other early attempts could be cited. To see occupational information as a special service or process of investigation is of comparatively recent origin.

The schools, as would be expected, were among the first to provide such service. Courses were offered and texts prepared to provide such information. Public agencies have also made an important contribution. The United States Bureau of Census publishes a classified Index of Occupations which classifies 451 occupations under 11 groupings. The United States Employment office published a *Dictionary of Occupational Titles,* commonly referred to as the D.O.T. This is probably the most widely accepted and used. The first publications of the employment service were published industry by industry. These were brought together in 1939 in the first edition of the *Dictionary of Occupational Titles* in five volumes. Trained job analysts went into hundreds of plants and business establishments and gathered information that described 17,452 separate jobs, known by 12,292 additional titles. A revised edition appeared in 1949 containing 22,029 different jobs, with 17,995 titles, or a total of 40,023. This time it appeared in two volumes; Volume I contains definitions of jobs found in America, alphabetically arranged, coded, and identified; Volume II contains such matters as the occupational classification structure, commodities sold in retail and wholesale trades, and a glossary of terms.

The classification divides the whole field into seven major occupational groups:

> Professional and Managerial Occupations
> Clerical and Sales Occupations
> Service Occupations
> Agricultural, Fishery, Forestry and Kindred
>   Occupations
> Skilled Occupations
> Semiskilled Occupations
> Unskilled Occupations

Each one is subdivided and coded for easy reference. Another volume or supplement is a compilation of Entry Occupations, or those occupations that can be entered without previous training and can lead to other occupations. The D.O.T. is no doubt the most extensive and has been used by many agencies other than the employment service, such as schools, libraries, and others who do vocational counseling.

Other agencies publish other material. The Bureau of Labor Statistics, in the United States Department of Labor, together with the Veterans Administration, publish an *Occupational Outlook Handbook*. The United States Employment Service publishes *Occupational Guides*. There are many other sources of information. Many books are available that describe occupations and their nature; articles in popular magazines sometimes describe specific jobs or areas of work; biographies and fiction often describe persons engaged in certain occupations and give a very lifelike presentation of the nature of the work. Many businesses and trade associations publish pamphlets and brochures. Some schools have developed elaborate systems for assembling and filing such information.

There are many means of disseminating occupational information.

——Personal conversation is one. In the interview the counselor can discuss vocational choice and its meaning for the individual.

——Much can be done in groups. Schools offer career courses by various titles. YMCA's, churches, and others often have series of discussions on vocations.

——Career days are a traditional program in many schools. Here representatives of various lines of endeavor present their own vocation.

——Many groups such as churches, Y's and others conduct recruiting conferences which are sources of information for special areas.

——Interviews can be planned with individuals who have had experience and success in certain fields.

——Field trips to various industries and institutions can be arranged. These enable a person to witness a job or operation and to ask questions of those participating in it.

——Visual aids are available in many lines of endeavor.

——Try out experiences, in the summer or after school hours, give an opportunity to gain information by firsthand experience.

Occupational information is of such importance that certain standards should govern its use. The texts on vocational guidance have included various lists. They naturally overlap and include much of the same material to emphasize the importance of understanding the nature of the work, the training required, and so forth. We have developed a list, which is in large part a compilation of those elements that are found in other volumes, but we have put them in the form of questions which an individual would need to ask in order to have thorough and complete information on which to base a vocational choice.

What is the background of the occupation?

What briefly is the history of the occupation?
What has been its chief contributions to society?

How is it viewed by others? by society in general?
Who have been some of its leaders? its greatest names?
Who are some of its chief exponents today?

What is the nature of the work?

If I choose this occupation, what will I do?
What will be the nature of the task I perform?
What responsibilities will I accept?
How will I spend my time 5, 6, or 7 days a week?

What personal qualifications are required?

What mental abilities are necessary?
What physical requirements are demanded?
What special aptitudes or skills are deemed necessary?

What training is required?

What are the educational requirements?
Does a person need a high school education? college education? advanced training?
Where is this training secured?
How long does it take?
What does it cost?

Who may enter the occupation?

Are there any restrictions as to age, sex, race, or religion?
Are special examinations required for this occupation, such as ordination into the ministry or acceptance into a union?
Does the state require licensing to practice this occupation?
Is it necessary to belong to an organization, (labor, religious, other) to enter or remain in the occupation?

What are the possibilities for employment?

Is the occupation overcrowded?
If I complete my training, will I be likely to find a job?
What are the trends for the future?

Do the opportunities for employment vary seasonally?

Are the possibilities for employment different in different parts of the country?

What are the working conditions?

Is the work monotonous or interesting?

Do I work alone or in a group?

What are the physical and emotional hazards?

Do I work indoors or out?

With whom will I be closely associated?

Do I travel or stay in one location?

Are the surroundings attractive or unattractive, pleasant or monotonous?

What are the hours? Is there much overtime?

What is the remuneration?

What is the average income?

What is the range in income?

What are the chances for advancement in income?

What is the security of the occupation?

What is the pension or retirement plan?

What are the insurance plans?

What are the fringe benefits, such as car allowance, extra fees, expense accounts, commissions, bonuses, and so forth.

Is housing provided?

What are the vacation arrangements?

What are the satisfactions and discouragements?

What is the status of the occupation?

What are the most satisfying aspects of the occupation?

What are its discouragements and frustrations?

What are the chances for advancement?

How will the occupation affect my personal life?

How could I view this occupation as a life career?

Is this an occupation in which I could see myself with respect?

Are there elements in the occupation that would cause me to compromise my moral principles?

How will this occupation affect my family life?

Is this an occupation in which my wife (fiancé, or husband) agrees?

Will it take me away from the home evenings, long periods of time?

Does this work tend to stimulate growth in character?

What is the value to society?

Does this occupation fill a real need in the world?

Does it provide a definite benefit to the good of man, the community, the world?

Principles of the Use of Occupational Information

There is often a misunderstanding that the use of occupational information merely consists of indiscriminate passing out of material. On the contrary, the use of occupational information is itself a specialized technique and certain principles should govern its use. Far from being a simple process it can at times be a very complex one with the possibility of doing actual harm.

The following principles would tend to eliminate the dangers and increase the effectiveness of occupational information services.

(1) It should be recognzied that no one can have all the occupational information that is necessary for all counselors. The new counselor may feel obligated to be able to answer all the questions about any profession or occupation. This is impossible; even the experienced counselor can not have

all this information. He does need to have a general understanding of the world of work, he needs to know the importance of occupational information, he needs to realize that it must be thorough and accurate. *He needs to know where to secure the information.* This is especially important for pastors and others who do vocational counseling part time. They do not need to know the details of all the occupations; they do need to know where information about them can be secured.

(2) Good occupational services do not consist in giving out facts but in helping the person find them for himself. Here as in all counseling the purpose is to help the person help himself so that guidance becomes a real learning experience.

(3) It should be recognized that information about vocations can be used in a variety of ways and for quite different purposes. Baer and Roeber list eight different functions of occupational information. They are:

(a) EXPLORATORY USES: Occupational information used to help the counselee to make an extensive study of the world's work or selected fields of occupations. . . .

(b) INFORMATIONAL USES: Occupational information used to aid the counselee make an intensive study of a few occupations. . . .

(c) ASSURANCE USES: Occupational information used by the counselee to assure himself that he has an appropriate choice of vocation or that he has abandoned an inappropriate vocational choice.

(d) ADJUSTIVE USES: Occupational information used to assist the counselee to gain the insight necessary to change attitudes and ultimately to change his plans from an inappropriate to an appropriate vocational choice.

(e) MOTIVATIONAL USES: Occupational information used to arouse the counselee's interest in schoolwork or in vocational planning.

(f) HOLDING USES: Occupational information used as a means of holding the counselee until he gains some insight into his real needs and into his behavior.

(g) EVALUATIVE USES: Occupational information used to check the accuracy and adequacy of the counselee's knowledge and understanding of an occupation or family of occupations.

(h) STARTLE USES: Occupational information used to see if a counselee shows signs of certainty or uncertainty after he chooses a particular vocation.[1]

(4) The giving of occupational information is a continuous process. The selection of a career is a process that takes time. The securing of occupational information is something that continues throughout the process. The student is continually securing information and growing in his understanding and application of that information.

(5) Occupational information is in a constant state of change. Technological changes, scientific discoveries, shifts in population, the depletion of natural resources, international relations, economic conditions—all such things change the nature, even the availability, of many occupations. For this reason, information about jobs must be in a constant state of revision. From all indications this will always be the case. The counselor, therefore, must always check his own experience against the most recent and most accurate information that is available and must always evaluate the material he recommends to someone else.

(6) Occupational information should be used with caution. Since far-reaching decisions are made on the basis of the information an individual has, every precaution should be taken

---

[1] Reprinted by permission from *Occupational Information* by Baer and Roeber. Copyright 1951 by Science Research Associates, Inc.

to be sure that the information is accurate and complete. It should also be recognized that in some areas information is necessarily incomplete. The counselor does not know for sure just what personality qualities are necessary to be successful in some lines of endeavor. Dogmatic or theoretical statements could be misleading in such a case.

(7) It should be recognized that there is a *readiness* for occupational information. Information about jobs has a value only when it coincides with a person's interest and maturity that enables him both to understand and use it.

(8) Requests for occupational information may or may not mean this is a student's major concern. A young person may express a desire to know more about an occupation when what he really wants to do is talk through his own uncertainty, his own feeling of inadequacy and concern. To give him the information, which he no doubt needs and is entitled to, may cause the counselor to feel he has solved a problem when he may have missed the real issue.

On the other hand, a lack of information may be the counselee's major problem; if this is true, to fail to make it available is equally serious.

(10) Occupational information, like testing, should be used in connection with all other methods of counseling and guidance. Some counselors oversimplify to the point of implying that giving accurate occupational information is good vocational guidance. Nothing could be farther from the truth. If a student has a warped or confused vocational objective, if he lacks understanding of himself, or is involved in emotional conflicts; no amount of occupational information will enable him to make a valid vocational choice, no matter how accurate or complete the information is.

Occupational information, like the findings of psychological tests, should be given in such a way that the individual has ample opportunity to express his feelings, to raise questions, and to work through his problems relative to the implications of that information to his own life.

In other words, occupational information must be used as a part of the counseling process.

Referral

The minister, religious educator, university chaplain, or university pastor is not trained in the special techniques of vocational counseling, such as psychological testing or occupational information. At times he must depend upon a referral.

It is a basic principle of all counseling or personnel work that no one should attempt to do something that someone else can do better. A referral is indicated when the pastor or religious worker does not have the time, the training, the resources, or the relationship that enables him to do a good and thorough job.

In fairness to his people he must make use of all the resources that are available. It borders on the unethical to guess at a student's aptitudes or abilities on matters that will affect his whole life career, when there are trained people who can secure accurate reliable information. It is unnecessary for a pastor to know everything about all the occupations, or to know what jobs are available in a community when there are people who do nothing else.

Sometimes the greatest service a pastor can render is to get people to the agency or the individual who can help the most. In order to do this he must be familiar with the resources in his own community. Preferably he should know these people personally. Some of the agencies with which he should be acquainted are:

Public Schools. The public school will be the pastor's most frequent contact in matters of vocational guidance. The schools have recognized their responsibility in the matter of vocational choice and training. Many schools provide a counseling and guidance department with people who have specialized in vocational guidance. Smaller schools depend on their administrative and teaching staff for such responsibilities. Almost all schools have some program of testing, sponsor career days, or include some courses on vocational planning.

Colleges and Universities. Any one working with students should be familiar with the services of the department of counseling and testing of the university. This is more and more an accepted part of every major university. Here a student may receive very thorough testing and counseling by people who are usually highly trained and qualified in the field of vocational guidance. This is also a source of referral for the pastor who wishes a battery of tests administered to a high school student or a young adult who is not in school. Most colleges will provide such services for a fairly modest fee.

Employment Service. The United States Employment service maintains local offices all over the country. Their purpose is to help people find jobs and to help employers find workers. They do both vocational counseling and testing, although the counseling that is done is usually brief and directed toward helping an individual find a job rather than work out a career as we have described it here. They also gather information about occupational trends, shortages, and needs. There are some private employment services that help people find a job on a fee basis.

Office of Vocational Rehabilitation. This is a service provided by the state with the assistance of the Federal Government, to assist the physically handicapped find useful work. Their services are based on a medical diagnosis for the purpose of determining the person's capacity to work and also if possible to eliminate or diminish the degree of the handicap. They provide individual counseling and specialized training, and assist in placement.

Social Agencies. Every pastor should know the social agencies in his community. Some can give specific help on vocational problems. The YMCA, YWCA, YMHA, sometimes provide vocational guidance services. One of the major responsibilities of The Urban League is the vocational guidance of Negro youth. Rescue Missions and the Salvation Army can find jobs for transients. Good Will Industries is an agency whose one purpose is to provide employment for the handicapped.

Personnel Workers in Industry. The nature of their services varies a great deal with the policy of the industry and the training of the worker. Some do little more than interview for possible employment. Some provide real vocational guidance utilizing testing and counseling techniques.

There are other cases in which a vocational problem will reveal such emotional maladjustment that referral to a psychiatrist will be necessary, or where physical factors related to vocational choice will indicate referral to a physician, but we are thinking here of those referral resources that have to do primarily with aid in vocational matters.

When a pastor makes a referral to a specialist or an agency, he does not break contact with the person. He still maintains a relationship as a pastor. There may be occasions when he helps the person find the best help available and the vocational counselor, or whoever it may be, assumes the major portion of the responsibility. There may be other situations where the pastor makes a referral for specific services such as a battery of tests, for example, but continues as the counselor. There may be other occasions where the vocational problem is related to a family problem or a religious problem and help is secured for the vocational aspect of the problem. Then the pastor continues as a family or religious counselor and the two men work co-operatively on the matter. In all cases the pastor has unique and distinctive points of view and a particular concern about his people. He has interests and concerns other than vocational so that in almost all cases he maintains a pastoral relationship whether or not he makes a referral.

Part II

The Minister
and
Vocational Counseling

V

THE MINISTER AND VOCATIONAL
GUIDANCE

Vocational guidance is now a separate profession with its own specialists, its own techniques, its own principles and procedures, its own literature, and its own training. It can rightly be called a movement. It numbers literally thousands of people who are trained and qualified as vocational counselors or vocational guidance workers.

In the light of all this should the minister even attempt to do vocational guidance? Some pastors would say "No." They take the position: "We are ministers, religion is our specialty and our responsibility. Let the vocational counselors handle the vocational problems."

Many vocational counselors would say "No." The minister, they would say, is not trained to do vocational guidance. He is not trained in vocational testing. He is not aware of job opportunities, or job requirements, or the other information necessary to make a wise vocational choice; therefore, it is better if he simply leaves it alone.[1]

There is some validity for this position. The pastor is not

---

[1] The one exception would be counseling for church vocations. Here they want the pastor to be a specialist. This is of such significance that it be discussed in a latter chapter.

a trained vocational counselor; he is not trained to give vocational tests and does not have technical information about job opportunities and requirements.

There is another sense in which the minister can't evade this responsibility. Sometimes because of his position as a pastor he finds himself with a vocational counseling situation thrust upon him.

(1) Young people come to him with their problems because he is their pastor. They have confidence in him. They feel he is interested in them. The vocational problem may be only one of many problems the young persons present but they present it to the pastor.

The vocational counselor has tools, techniques, and occupational information the pastor doesn't have; but the pastor has a relationship the vocational counselor doesn't have. The relationship may be more important than the tools and techniques and occupational information.

The pastor may want to utilize the insights of the vocational counselor, he may want to refer to a vocational counselor, for all or part of the process; even so, he still wants to maintain a relationship as a pastor with the young persons.

(2) The pastor has a responsibility in vocational guidance because many of the problems that are brought to him as a pastor may have vocational implications.

Here, for example, is a young man who goes to his pastor with what seems to be a vocational problem. He is an engineering major but isn't happy in it. His grades are acceptable but he would like to go into education. He wants to work with young people. This is obviously an educational and vocational problem. Why doesn't the pastor send him to the vocational counselors who can look at his aptitude tests, check his educational qualifications, give him some vocational interest tests and help him decide what he ought to do? Why didn't he go to the university counselors in the first place? Because this is only part of the problem. As he states the problem, "Dad just doesn't understand. He's an engineer, my uncle is an engineer. He has always wanted me to enter his firm. He says it's silly to work for what school teachers get. He just can't understand that I don't want to be an engineer."

The pastor knows the family. He knows the father. The boy thought of him.

There is a truism in counseling that we do not counsel problems, we counsel persons. The persons may have many sides to their problems—some personal, some educational, some vocational, some spiritual, and all interrelated. Because a pastor is constantly counseling persons, some of them will have problems, like this boy's, which was as much a family problem as it was vocational. In such cases the pastor can not say, "I'll discuss your family problem but not the vocational problem." The vocational problem is a part of the family problem. The pastor must deal with the whole thing.

Sometimes these situations can be quite severe and disturbing to a young person. Here is the statement of a young man who is interested in music. He feels he would like to make it his vocation. His parents think this is foolish. He says,

I feel sick and miserable when thinking of my future. . . . My mother believes teaching is a respectable and needed occupation. Sometimes she tries to drive me into it. . . . I want to be a musician. But I'm scared to tell her. She always laughs when I am serious. I hate her for trying to force me into her plans. I don't want to hate her. She's really good and I love her honestly. . . .[2]

Let us assume the young man brought this problem to his pastor, for it is the kind of problem that very commonly is taken to ministers. The pastor has much to contribute. He

[2] Strang, op. cit., p. 410.

can not give the music aptitude tests to determine whether or not music is a realistic choice but he can do much to work out the relationship with the mother which may be a more basic problem. However, he can not deal with this relationship without dealing with the problem of vocational choice which is what, at the present, at least, destroys the relationship. Here he has some advantages. He knows the family. He has access to the home. He has perhaps worked with them on other occasions and has their confidence. Once the family problem has been alleviated, the vocational problem is still present and still needs to be solved. He can, and no doubt should, use referral for certain information and perhaps for continued counseling but if the problem is brought to him he can not dodge his responsibility.

Not all complications involve the family. Sometimes the problem is moral or ethical. A young man in a fairly successful business is required by his employer to do certain things which seem to be questionable. They are not illegal, but they are slightly deceitful. They seem in contradiction to the Christian ethics and Christian ideals. He doesn't discuss it with his boss. He discusses it with his pastor. In the conversation he raises these questions. "Should I change jobs?" "What should I do?" "This is really all I know. If I change jobs, what should I change to?" "Is it worth going back to school? If so, what school should I go to?" These are questions with far-reaching implications which face the pastor in the field of vocational guidance, at least, to some degree.

(3) A whole movement of vocational guidance has developed, and while the schools have done much in this area, there still aren't enough vocational counselors to go around. Many times a pastor will be confronted by a person with a vocational problem and no sources of referral.

This is especially true in small schools and rural areas. Not many rural schools have vocational counselors on their staffs. The guidance that is done is done by teachers who already have a full load of teaching and co-curricular activities. They do not have either the time or the specialized training necessary to qualify them for counseling.[3] This situation is true not only in rural areas and small schools. Some larger school systems with good staffs cannot help all the students in a thorough and adequate way. Because a school has a guidance department and specialists on the staff does not mean that all the pupils are getting adequate vocational guidance. This is in no sense a criticism. Those who are active in the vocational guidance field are the first to admit this fact. Humphreys and Traxler, in their book *Guidance Services*, written for school counselors, state:

Lest we become complacent we should note two points: First, vast numbers of schools in the United States have *no planned systematic guidance of any kind*. And second, all too many schools that *profess to give educational and vocational* guidance to their pupils have programs that fall *short of the mark*. In fact, objective observation indicates that it is the *rare* public school or college that has fully adequate services for evaluating and for otherwise assisting individual students.[4]

These are statements of men who are active in the vocational guidance movement and who believe in it. They are in a position to know what the situation is. What it says to the pastor is obvious. Unless he is in one of these *rare* communities where the program is fully adequate, of necessity he may have to work in this area.

In addition to this, there are thousands of older young

[3] Jane Warters says in *High School Personnel Work Today,* "Three-fourths of our high schools are too small to be able to afford the services of the guidance specialist."

[4] Reprinted by permission from *Guidance Services* by Humphreys and Traxler. Copyright 1954 by Science Research Associates, Inc.

people who are through school and are drifting blindly in their vocational life, dissatisfied and unhappy and with no one to whom to turn, for very few private agencies offer vocational guidance.[5] If these young people come to the pastor, he cannot escape some feeling of responsibility. He is confronted with a situation in which, like it or not, he must do something about vocational guidance.

(4) If there are religious implications to vocational choice, then the pastor has something to say that no one else is saying. The vocational guidance movement has done far more than the church in recognizing the significance of vocational choice. It has made the church aware of the problem and has offered many insights and helpful techniques. Only rarely in the books on vocational guidance is reference made to the religious or spiritual implications of vocational choice. In fact, many of the publications on vocational guidance do not seem to grasp the significance of the word "vocation" in its original or deepest sense at all—as a "calling".

There is a new interest in the word "vocation" these days. Elton Trueblood puts it this way:

One of the heartening developments of our time has been the growing awareness, on the part of those touched by the Christian gospel, of the meaning of vocation. The idea is that God can call us to many kinds of activity and that secular work well done is a holy enterprise.[6]

This concept of vocation as a calling is not found in the texts on vocational guidance.

Speaking as a religious educator, Nevin Harner says,

[5] We are not ignoring employment services. They do offer vocational guidance but primarily they find employment rather than give extended vocational guidance.
[6] Trueblood, *Your Other Vocation* (New York: Harper & Brothers, 1952), p. 58. Used by permission.

There is vocational guidance, and beyond that there is *Christian* vocational guidance. The Church has something to say to youth as they face their life careers which the public school or a guidance bureau cannot say explicitly and fully. It has a divine plan of life to hold before their eyes. It has the Christian ideal of service to throw into their calculations, as they try to find the niche in which they will spend their lives. It has all the needs of all mankind the world around to bring home to them. This is the unique task of the Church in vocational guidance. How much of the rest it does will depend upon what other agencies in the community are doing, but this is its own peculiar specialty.[7]

Hoover Rupert stresses a similar thought when he says the service motive should permeate all vocational activity.

In a world gone secularly mad we need to bring the sanity of a vocational philosophy which recognizes the potential sacredness of all useful work. In a world which worships at the shrine of business and financial success as primary factors in vocational selection, we need to sound the summons to the service motives in all vocations.[8]

With this most religious leaders would agree but it is only fair to recognize the fact that thus far the church has made such statements only in general terms. There has been little attempt to train pastors or religious educators in the methods and techniques by which such Christian vocational guidance is done. The texts on pastoral counseling or religious education do not make any significant contribution at this point.

Thus the vocational guidance movement has developed the methods and techniques but may not go as far as the church would like in emphasizing some of the implications of "vocation." The church on the other hand, has spoken of the prin-

[7] Harner, *Youth Work in the Church* (Nashville: Abingdon Press, 1943), p. 93. Used by permission.

[8] *Pastoral Care*, edited by J. Richard Spann (Nashville: Abingdon Press, 1951), p. 93. Used by permission.

ciple but has failed to develop the practical methods and to train its religious workers in the means whereby it is done.

Another emphasis should be included here. If vocational choice is as important as we have said it is, that is, if it is one of the two or three most far-reaching decisions an individual will ever make, it is a decision that should be made only in a framework of prayer and worship. This is not the place to discuss the validity of prayer. Unless one accepts that it has some value, of course, then this would be considered unnecessary. We are assuming that pastors and most vocational counselors do believe in prayer. Belief in the power of prayer does not minimize the importance of aptitude tests or any other methods or techniques. It does recognize that man is a spiritual being and as such has a resource that helps in making life's decisions. Here the pastor's position is unique. It empowers him to help his young people recognize the importance of making all decisions, vocational and otherwise, in a spirit of prayer and furthermore to give them such help as will enable them to do it. Frequently the church has said men ought to pray and yet has never taken the pains to show them how. Whether or not the pastor does anything else in vocational guidance, he should help the young person surround his efforts to make a good vocational choice with a spirit and practice of prayer and worship.

The pastor is not and should not attempt to be a specialist in vocational guidance. He has neither the time nor the training for that. The counseling he does in the vocational area is done as a part of his general counseling. The problems that are brought to him come because of his position as a pastor and because of his relationship with his people and they should be seen as such. The pastor functions as a pastoral counselor, not a specialized vocational counselor. He is not a marriage counselor either, in the specialized sense. However, by virtue of the fact that he is a pastor, he cannot help counseling with some people who have family problems. His position in relation to family problems is recognized much more readily than it is in relation to vocational problems, but it is the same.

The pastor, therefore, must know the basic principles of vocational guidance, something of the psychology of work, and the meaning it has in life. This is the purpose of the first section of this book.

A knowledge of certain basic principles, such as that vocational choice is a process that takes much time and that the vocational decision must always be the person's own, saves the pastor from making mistakes. The warnings of the vocational counselors must be heeded. The pastor must not make snap judgments about a person's aptitudes or abilities. He must not use inadequate information, or let a young person make a decision about a vocation without full knowledge of what the decision implies. To let a person make a wrong decision because the information was faulty or incomplete is almost inexcusable when accurate information is available.

The pastor must recognize his own limitations and the value of the services of others. He is not expected to give mental or vocational tests. This is a task for the specialist who has had the necessary training. He is not expected to have all the "occupational information" that will answer the questions any young person might raise. The pastor must know that there are people who have such skills and such information and if he knows these source people personally, he can work with them effectively. It is unfortunate that some pastors are unaware of or minimize the contributions that those who are trained in giving vocational tests and vocational guidance can render.

In some cases the pastor may utilize the services of a specialist in vocational testing; in some cases he may work co-operatively with the school guidance department in the interest of one of his young people; in some cases, of necessity he may handle the problem alone; but in all cases he should be aware of the importance of these sources to the individual. In a very real sense he is sharing in the destiny of the counselee and so he must make every effort that his counseling and guidance are thorough, complete, and competent.

VI

THE MINISTER COUNSELING

ON

PROBLEMS OF VOCATIONAL

ADJUSTMENT

The problem of adolescence is vocational choice. The problem of the adult is vocational adjustment.

The vocational guidance movement has been concerned primarily with vocational choice. It is only recently that it has begun to pay attention to vocational adjustment.

The adolescent may appeal to guidance workers in the schools for help. These counselors and teachers can give tests; they organize guidance classes; they sponsor career conferences; and help in many other ways with the matter of vocational choice. The church through its youth groups, summer conferences and camps often provides the opportunity to discuss the question of vocational choice.

The man in his forties, however, is not in school. He does not have a guidance counselor to whom he may go, he does not have a class in school or church in which to discuss such matters. Yet vocational problems may be one of his most serious concerns.

Let us take a hypothetical case of a man we will call John. While this story is not about a specific person, still it is based on fact. It can be duplicated in many case records and John could live in almost any community.

John is a member of the church. In fact, he would be considered active. He attends, he gives, he serves on the board, he has taken his turn on several committees. He and the pastor have been friendly although John has never discussed any of his personal matters with his pastor. It never seemed necessary before. Now, however, he is disturbed. He feels that he must talk to somebody, so he drops by the church office.

It is obvious to the pastor that John is exhibiting considerable tension. The pastor knows that John is a salesman for a large firm and must travel quite a bit. He seems to be doing quite well in his work. The problem he presents is this. The position of regional sales manager of his firm is to be open soon. John is in line by tenure and sales record for the position. He has just heard indirectly that he is not going to be promoted. He is angry. He is tempted to quit his job and get into another type of work.

John has been with his present company for almost ten years. Before that he had worked for several companies, he had sold advertising, operated a drill press, worked as a claim adjuster and in several part-time positions. Except for his present position he has never stayed with any one company very long. He expressed dissatisfaction with something in almost all of the other jobs. He enjoys his present job but is very critical of his boss who, he feels, is playing favorites and is discriminating against him.

John is married and has two children. His wife is a little younger than he and is a former school teacher. She graduated from college and taught school for several years. He feels she misses the teaching and the extra income she had before the children were born. She feels if he would be more aggressive and stand up to his boss, he could get more recognition and advancement.

Although his salary is adequate, they have not been able to secure the kind of housing they would like or to afford the kind of cars, vacations, and so forth, that some of their friends have. He would like to belong to the country club but she reminds him that they can't afford it. If he got this promotion, it might be possible.

John is a pleasant person and has many friends, yet he is sometimes opinionated and expresses strong likes and dislikes. This has been true in the committees at the church and the pastor suspects it is true on the job also.

John finished high school but never went to college, a fact that he regrets. He frequently states that he always intended to and wishes now that he had.

He admits that he is mad "clear through." He feels that he has had a raw deal. "You work your head off for a company," he says, "and what does it get you? They pass you by for some punk kid with a college degree."

What he'd really like to do, he says, is "walk out and tell them they can have their lousy job. But what would I do then? I'm not trained for anything else.

"If I had it to do over again, I'd go to college and get a degree, then I could tell some other guys where to go. I've even thought about it—I've heard about other fellows who went back to school, but my wife isn't satisfied with our income now. I don't know what we'd do for the four years I was in school.

"I guess I'm just a failure. I've got to do something. I suppose I could stick it out, but it's pretty tough when you think you're getting gypped. Do you think I ought to quit?

"Do you think it would be silly to go back to school? You

know my wife, how do you think she would take it? Maybe if I calmed down some, I could go and talk to the boss.

"I hate to bother you with this, Preacher; I know how busy you are, but I had to talk to somebody. What do you think I should do?"

John's case is, in no sense, a unique one. The details may be different, but the dissatisfaction is not.

The studies that have been made would indicate that such dissatisfaction is rather widespread. A recent Gallup poll disclosed that nearly 50% of all the persons they surveyed were unhappy in their work. A study of over 1,000 young adults found that three fourths were dissatisfied with their vocations and would have preferred to be working at something different. A survey of 700 adults found that over 52% said that if they could live their lives over again, they would have chosen another vocation.

This is a tragic picture. Such figures represent a tremendously large amount of discouragement, frustration, and defeat. Such attitudes inevitably cloud all of life itself.

Many of these people come to the pastor. One reason is that they have nowhere else to go. The young person is in school, the school provides programs and personnel to assist him with his choice. The man who is dissatisfied with his job, who finds no meaning or purpose in his work can discuss it with his wife, he can talk it over with his friends, even his boss, but he has no one to whom he can go for counsel and guidance. Industry provides personnel workers who can be very helpful but they are still psychologically identified with the management; and the man in a small business or the man in business for himself or the man in one of the professions has no such worker. This is not a medical problem, although it can have obvious physical implications. The majority do not need a psychiatrist, they are not mentally ill, but they are discouraged, dissatisfied, unhappy, troubled, and confused. The pastor is one man with whom they can talk, not necessarily because they think of him as a vocational counselor, but because he is available and he can try to understand.

Also such problems come to the pastor because they are often, if not always, related to something else—family difficulties, moral questions, feelings of guilt or failure. These are things a pastor deals with all the time.

Whether a person comes to discuss a vocational problem that turns out to be basically a family problem, or whether he comes to discuss a family problem that has real vocational implications is not the important matter. In either case, the pastor deals with the "whole person." He doesn't counsel problems, he counsels persons—but it is well for him to know some of the principles and some of the factors that underlie vocational satisfaction and dissatisfaction.

The truth of the matter is that not much is known about this subject even yet. It needs to be the basis of much more study and investigation although some principles are recognized.

First of all, vocational satisfaction or dissatisfaction is relative. What is satisfying to one is monotonous to another. The counselor must avoid any preconceived ideas, or the projecting of his own feelings, his own likes or dislikes onto the counselee.

Teaching school, for one person may be challenging and exciting. As he sees youth grow and develop through the formative years of life, he feels a real sense of fulfillment and purpose. For another, teaching may be dull and monotonous, a repetition of the same material year after year and a constant struggle with "little brats" he can't control. Work that requires extensive travel for one may be exciting and enjoyable; for another who prefers to stay at home it is unpleasant and discouraging. Work that is done in the quiet and solitude of a laboratory provides for some men the very atmosphere which gives them the greatest satisfactions. Gregarious personalities who want to be associated with groups of persons would find it most unsatisfactory.

What is routine to one may be creative to another. What is enjoyable to one may be nerve-racking to another. Vocational satisfaction must always be seen in terms of the individual and his needs.

Job satisfaction is not necessarily the same as enjoying one's work. Many persons who like to do the things required by their occupations are dissatisfied with their jobs because of inadequate pay, the social position of the job, or the conditions or surroundings of the work. Here is a man who was superintendent of schools in a small town—an important position. He did his work well, but he quit his job to sell chicken feed. Why? Not because he didn't like his work, he did; but so that he could put his children through college. He had a more adequate income selling chicken feed than he did teaching school.

Some occupational dissatisfaction may be due to poor vocational choice in the first place. Some vocational counselors feel that a large percentage of the population not only choose jobs for which they are not fitted but do not choose the occupations they really prefer. They feel that a large proportion of young people do not have the self-understanding or the understanding of their world that is necessary for making the best choice for them. If this is true, it points out the inadequacy of our vocational guidance and training.

With some their dissatisfaction may be the result of an inability to do the job. They have been selected and placed in positions that demand more ability than they possess. They are constantly under pressure and strain. They are behind in their work and subject to criticism by their superiors. Dissatisfaction is the inevitable result. The only solution is to find employment that is within the limits of their capacity and provides some opportunity for success.

With others the opposite is true. Their occupation does not require or use the abilities they have. It leaves them unchallenged and thus bored and unhappy. Vocational satisfaction depends not only on having enough ability to do the necessary tasks, but in being challenged to use the maxim of one's potential. Only when he is challenged and has the opportunity of being creative, will the person of high ability find satisfaction.

Probably the largest single cause of job dissatisfaction is poor interpersonal relations. Job satisfaction depends not only on the ability to do the job but on the ability to get along with one's co-workers. People are happiest and find the greatest satisfactions in life when their relations with other people are friendly and enjoyable. This is true in a neighborhood, a home, a church, a club or organization, and on the job.

In any position there are some who are in authority and some who are not. There are relationships with fellow workers within a plant or colleagues on a faculty; there are relationships with customers, clients, students, patients, parishioners, as the case may be. To be satisfied in one's work, one must have meaningful and satifying relationships with all such persons.

In all fields there are status systems. They vary with the culture and the nature of the work, but they are always there. Individuals who have difficulty with authority figures, who are jealous of the ones with whom they are working or competing, who cannot respect or who do not have a real appreciation for the ones they work for are bound to be dissatisfied. For example, the teacher who is fascinated by English literature but doesn't like children is not going to enjoy teaching English literature. A man may be an excellent machinist but if he can't get along with his fellow workers and feels great hostility toward his boss, he will not enjoy his job. A social worker who has great compassion for the underprivileged and down-trodden but can not get along with her colleagues and has a great fear of her superiors will probably change from one agency to another frequently.

Job satisfaction is also related to the concept of the self. Super agrees with Schaffer's hypothesis that "if a man or woman cannot, in his working life, find opportunities to be the kind of person he wants to be, for self-fulfillment, he will be dissatisfied with his work." In Super's words, "Jobs serve to implement self-concepts."[1] When the concept of self and the occupational role are in conflict, dissatisfaction is bound to result; on the other hand, if the work one does or the position one holds enables him to play the kind of role that is in line with the self-concept that he wants to assume, then satisfaction is very likely. In other words, when a man's job provides outlets for his personal needs and values, it is a career for him which provides satisfaction and meaning. If one's occupation permits a man to be the kind of person he wants to be, it is a good occupation for him. Those who do not find their needs satisfied, those who because of their work are forced to play roles that are contrary to their preferred concepts of themselves will be unhappy in their work.

The man who conceives of himself as something of a scholar, but has to do manual labor, for example, or the man who can find employment only as a typist but sees this as a feminine task will not find satisfaction in his work no matter how well paid he is. Sometimes a job may force a person into conflicting roles, such as the school counselor who is asked to serve also

[1] Super: *op. cit.*, p. 183.

in administrative and at times disciplinary matters, the businessman who finds himself in competition with a close friend, or the college president who is by nature a scholar but is expected to be a fund raiser.

On occasion job dissatisfaction may be due to ethical implications. Here is an older man who has been out of work for some time. Because of his age and limited training, the job opportunities are few. Finally he is given a chance to work at something of which he morally disapproves. Twenty years earlier he would not have considered such a possibility. Now he and his family need the money. What should he do? He has been an active church man, so he takes the problem to his pastor.

A young man presents a similar problem. He is a repair man in a radio and television shop. What he is doing is not wrong but at times it borders on it. He tells his pastor, "We use inferior material. We do jobs we know won't last. We overcharge. How can I reconcile this with my ideals?" he asks. "I could quit but what could I do then? I need the work."

These are real problems. There really is no place for such persons to go—unless it is to the pastor.

Job satisfaction is the result of a combination of a number of things—the ability to do the work with a reasonable degree of success, the feeling that one's abilities are being challenged, the ability to get along with others, need for accord with one's concept of himself, a sense of worth in the work, and perhaps many other related factors.

The pastor has a special place here. He is a counselor first of all and counseling in this area is basically no different from counseling in any other. His purposes are essentially the same. The pastor's task primarily is to create an atmosphere of acceptance and understanding that enables a person to think through his feelings about his problem, drain off his emotions, weigh the alternatives in an objective and nonthreatening atmosphere. It is through such a procedure that the counselee comes to a clearer and better understanding of himself, better insight into the situation, and some basis by which to make a decision if a decision is necessary.

The vocational problem may be interrelated to family problems, religious problems, or personal feelings of failure and unworthiness that may or may not be related to his job. Whatever the problem, the pastor listens, accepts, understands. Clearing up a family involvement may help the counselee adjust on the job. Helping him find a better vocational adjustment may free him for the better handling of some other aspects of his life. Improvement in any area of experience helps all areas.

Concern in this study is with those aspects that are primarily vocational or highly involved with vocational life. Here the pastor is concerned about the man's (or woman's) attitudes, his feelings towards his work. He listens as the counselee pours out his feelings of futility on the job, his hostility toward his boss, his sense of uselessness about his achievements or questions the advisibility of making a change. This is a slow process but gradually he dispels the negative emotions and the counselee can come to a place of understanding and decision.

At times the pastor is an interpreter. Some people need to have certain facts about vocational life interpreted to them. In marriage counseling the texts are stressing more and more the fact that couples ought to be prepared for some conflict; that some disagreement, some conflict in marriage is normal and even wholesome. At least it should not come as a surprise or cause the husband or wife to panic and feel that this is not necessarily a good marriage.

The same principle applies in the vocational field. People

need to realize that there are some discouragements in every vocation. There is probably no position but what has some elements that are uninteresting and some that may be unpleasant. Even the most exciting and glamorized vocations have aspects that are monotonous and commonplace.

Sometimes a person expects too much. Recruiters (including those who recruit for the ministry) are partly to blame for this. The competition for topflight personnel is so keen that in an effort to persuade young people to select a particular profession the attractive and glamorous aspects are often overplayed.

People also need to recognize that satisfaction with one's work can sometimes be acquired. Interest often follows experience. People can grow in an occupation so that what once was unpleasant may actually become enjoyable. Satisfaction is largely a matter of attitudes and these attitudes as someone has said, "do not depend upon having anything we want but in learning to enjoy what we have." This applies in the vocational life as well as in any other.

The pastor should be familiar with the sources of referral. This would include psychiatrists and mental health clinics, when the emotional disturbance is severe, or those agencies which deal specifically with vocational problems, such as the ones mentioned in an earlier chapter.

Some people are not going to find satisfaction in their jobs. They are in positions that are monotonous and filled with drudgery and any activity that is creative and satisfying will need to be found outside of work. This emphasizes the importance of avocations. It is essential that a person shall experience the joy and satisfaction of doing something worthwhile some place, if not through his vocation, then through his avocation. Granted this may be a poor substitute for a challenging vocation, yet it is better than none.

Vocational guidance is of prime importance now. In the future, as the work week decreases and leisure time increases, as the belt-line methods of production increase, avocational guidance will become significant.

The principles are essentially the same. Avocational counseling must take into account individual differences; it must be within the realm of a person's interest and abilities. It does not tell a person what he ought to do with his leisure time, but helps him find that which is best for him.

This is where church work comes into the picture. There is real meaning in the term "church work" for the layman. When a pastor can enlist a man in a genuine program of evangelism, stewardship, education, or any of the other numerous tasks that need to be done in every church, he is doing more than strengthening the program of the church; he is also doing something for the man. If the task is challenging and real, it enables a man to make a contribution of himself, his time, his energy, his talents. In a real sense this, too, is helping him to find and fulfill his vocation, using the word in the sense in which it was tended to be used as a "calling." The layman can be called to his field of service in and through the church as much as the man in the pulpit. Every pastor can think of persons who, as laymen, have rendered a vital contribution to the church and have thus found a sense of fulfillment in their own lives.

A man's work in the world is expressed not only through his job. When the Bible speaks of service, it refers to this total impact of a man's life. Who knows the good Samaritan's occupation in life? His service was the help he rendered to the man by the side of the road.

Amos was a sheepherder and dresser of sycamore trees. That was his occupation but not his greatest contribution. Paul was a tentmaker by trade and he practiced this trade through the years but that wasn't his vocation, his calling. His greatest work was for the Church of Jesus Christ.

The minister needs to keep before his people the truth that the greatest satisfactons of life come from a life of service. Sometimes this can be expressed in the way one earns his living—but it is much wider than this. IIe must also stress to his people the concept of life vocation—a total life of service. But it is not enough merely to proclaim this truth unless he helps the individual who is struggling to find out how he can express it in his life, in terms of his abilities and his opportunities. This takes personal work, counseling, and guidance.

Not all vocational dissatisfaction is bad. It can be discouraging but it can also be a means toward growth. As a young person is floundering in a job, he is really finding himself, as an older person is struggling with some problem, he can be led to a life of deeper understanding, fuller satisfaction and wider service if guidance is handled properly. To help in such a situation is the pastor's high privilege.

VII

GUIDANCE FOR CHURCH

VOCATIONS

Guidance for church vocations is an area of vocational guidance that is much larger and more complex than many people realize. In fact, the term "church vocations" represents a whole family of vocations which includes a wide variety of expressions and a large number of persons. The three most familiar are the minister, the director of religious education, and the missionary. Actually each one of these can be divided into several different specialties. The missionary, for example, could be a medical missionary, an evangelistic missionary, a missionary nurse or social worker, a missionary agriculturalist, a builder, or administrator.

John Oliver Nelson of Yale University has developed a chart of *Occupational Fields in Protestant and Orthodox Churches* in America which includes forty-eight different categories. They include, in addition to the familiar ones mentioned above: associate minister; minister of music; director of youth work; director of children's work; deaconess; church social worker; denominational executive; editor and lesson writer; expert in radio, films, and TV; religious publishing house manager; Council of Churches executive; institutional chaplain; weekday church school teacher; campus chaplain; college professor of religion; theological school professor; military chaplain; worker in church institutions—homes for children, old people, etc.; worker in church social service agencies; overseas relief worker. The estimated numbers participating in such vocations ranges from 130,000 who are serving as ministers in local churches to 20 who are serving as specialists in radio and TV.[1]

To stress the importance of the work these people are doing is but to say the obvious. The problems of our day are moral and spiritual problems. The need for a strong vital church is perhaps greater today than it has been for generations. Thousands of individuals who look to their religious leaders for personal and spiritual help emphasize the importance of securing, guiding, and training qualified, dedicated persons for the church vocations. It is no reflection on the laity when Dr. Nelson states in *An Enlistment Manual for Church Vocations*, "In a very real sense the future of the Church of Christ depends more on the personnel of its leaders than on any other factor." Where does the major responsibility lie? Who is most qualified for this highly important task?

The Unique Position of the Pastor

The vocational guidance movement in a relatively brief period of time has developed into a specialty with its own experts, its own techniques and principles, its own literature and training. Two questions arise: 1. Should counseling for church vocations be done by professional, trained vocational counselors? 2. Should pastors who are not trained as vocational counselors attempt to do counseling for church vocations? The answer to the first question is both "Yes" and "No." The

[1] Cf. Nelson: *Opportunities in Protestant Religious Vocations* (New York: Vocational Guidance Manual, 1952), p. 12ff.

vocational counselor can do a good job in this area provided he understands the nature of the ministry. Even so, there are not enough vocational counselors to go around. The answer to the second question is "Yes," with certain provisions, provided the pastor understands the nature of such counseling and is aware of all the principles involved.

In fact, the pastor is in a position which almost of necessity forces him into such a role. The pastor symbolizes the ministry to his young people. It is only natural when they think of one of the church vocations as a possible lifework they think of their own pastor. Several studies have been made of the factors or influences which caused young people to enter the ministry; results show that, almost without exception, the two strongest influences were the home and the local pastor.[2]

These studies also show that the young person went first to his pastor, not to the vocational counselor to talk about this problem; in fact, vocational counselors and public school teachers were of only negligible influence in the majority of cases.

The parents of young people who are considering the ministry or the mission field or some other area of church vocations are both interested and at times concerned. They, too, frequently want to discuss it with someone. They are likely to contact the pastor.

Many young people who consider the ministry or the mission field are in rural schools or in schools where there is no vocational counselor available. Where else can they go but to their pastor?

An increasing number of those interested in the ministry are older young people who have already completed school and

[2] Lest pastors get too satisfied with such a statement it should be pointed out that such influences can work both ways. The studies also show that one of the strongest determining factors or influences that tend to keep young people out of the ministry is also the local pastor.

are engaged in business or one of the professions. One study of 1500 theological students found that one third were through school when they made their decision to enter the ministry. About six per cent were in one of the professions when they reached such a decision. They have no vocational counselor to go to even if they so desire.[3]

That this is borne out in experience is attested to by at least one research project which inquired into the experience of a group of theological students, representing different denominations.

Furthermore, vocational counselors themselves encourage pastoral counseling at this point. Vocational counselors, in the main, do not want pastors doing vocational guidance except in the field of guidance for church vocations. They want the pastor to be the specialist here. Vocational counselors do not know denominational differences. They are not familiar with educational requirements for the ministry, with qualifications for ordination, with job opportunities, so in this area they want to refer to the pastor.

Vocational counselors do have certain reservations. They want the pastor to be trained in counseling and educational procedures. They hope he will use guidance principles and not exert undue pressure on the candidate but with such reservations they feel that this is a task for which the pastor is uniquely fitted.

Advantages

The pastor has many advantages for such a task. His very availability is one. All counseling depends on the availability of the counselor. The pastor is available to the young person or his family for both formal scheduled interviews and infor-

[3] Cf. Samuel Southard, *Counseling for Church Vocations* (Nashville: Broadman Press, 1957).

mal questions or conversations, such as those that take place after a youth meeting or at a social function. Sometimes some very effective counseling takes place on such an occasion.

As stated earlier, all effective vocational guidance depends upon first understanding the individual and, second, understanding the world of work. The pastor has a unique advantage in both of these areas.

When the young person is a member of the church, and this is usually though not always the case, the pastor knows the family background, he is familiar with its attitudes, its interests, its outlook. He may have ministered to the family in time of illness or difficulty; perhaps he has worked with them on boards or committees and in various activities of the church. He has had a chance to observe the young person in groups, to see him in social gatherings, to note how he relates to people, how he accepts responsibility, and to get some evidence of his real interest in the church. These are opportunities the vocational counselor usually does not have.

Then, too, the pastor knows the ministry. The vocational counselors make much of what they term "occupational information" and rightfully so. A decision to enter the ministry should not be made except on the basis of information that is thorough, accurate, and up to date. One of the problems in church vocations has been the fact that many have made this decision without a realization of all that it meant or of all that was involved.

The pastor himself is probably the greatest single source of occupational information about the church vocations. Good occupational information should not be limited to word of mouth or to one man's opinion. Material should be put in the hands of the candidate so that he can study and evaluate as he considers his decision. The material should answer questions and give guidance.

There has been a great gap at this point. Vocational counselors have developed a great deal of material on occupations in general, especially the professions. They have worked out strict and meaningful standards and principles. They have done very little on the church vocations.

It has been left to the churches to develop material on the church vocations. This they have done, but in the main it has been long on persuasion and short on information. Most of the material prepared thus far has been recruitment material, not guidance material. Only recently have we begun to get material that could be classified as guidance in nature and purpose. Occupational information for the church vocations should measure up to the same high standards required in other professions; it should be thorough, complete, and accurate. Again it is the pastor who is familiar with such material and who is the one who can and should make it available.

One of the misfortunes is that much of this information never reaches the young person who is not active in the church. It would be well if Councils of Churches could develop some interdenominational material and make it available to schools and colleges.

The pastor knows the whole range of church vocations. Many young persons who do not wish to enter the preaching ministry or go to the mission field have high aptitudes in music, drama, writing, or some such field and feel called to a religious vocation. They could be helped to find an area of service by consulting their pastor who is aware that such positions exist and can help them find the training that will be most helpful.

One of the reasons vocational counselors do not want to get involved in counseling on church vocations is that Protestantism is divided into such a wide variety of denominations. This problem is not present in other areas of vocational guidance. The young man considering one of the other professions such as education, law, or medicine, does not find his field divided into over 200 different groups, each with its own requirements for a degree, each with its own schools, and each with its own standards and qualifications. A vocational counselor cannot be expected to know all of these denominational differences. It is difficult enough for the pastor but at least he can be familiar with the requirements of his own group.

Closely allied with this is the training that is required. An important part of all vocational guidance is helping the individual secure the best training available. Again it is an area in which the pastor has the most experience. This has to do with more than denominational differences. It is also important to know what training is required for each of the church vocations and where it can be secured. A young man will follow quite a different procedure if he is preparing for the pastoral ministry, for missionary service, for the chaplaincy of a penal institution, or for religious journalism, for example. These are areas in which vocational counselors have only limited information and in which the pastor should be thoroughly familiar.

The pastor is the one most qualified to interpret the "call to the ministry." This is perhaps the only area of vocations where this is true. One enters the other professions such as teaching, law, or medicine and he may do so with great conviction and commitment. However, it is only to the ministry that he is expected to be "called." Much confusion and not a little anxiety exists at this point. It is not surprising that many vocational counselors shy away from such a discussion. It has an air of the mystical or the esoteric about it.

The pastor has a further advantage in that he has right at hand many opportunities to permit the young person to gain experience in church work on a volunteer basis. This has a double value. It enables the pastor to observe the young person in a position of leadership and responsibility and it enables the young person to get some understanding of the nature of the task.

Vocational counselors make much of the value of what they term "try-out" experiences. George Myers, a specialist in vocational guidance, speaks of the value of such experiences from the vocational counselor's point of view. He says, "One who samples the fundamental experiences of an occupation knows more about his aptitudes and limitations with reference to that occupation and sometimes with reference to an entire group of related occupations, than he could possibly learn in any other way."[4]

There are few professions that have such natural facilities available whereby the young person can actually participate in the work, get something of the "feel" of it without engaging in it professionally. The motives for such activities should always be those of service but there are by-products that are of great importance from the standpoint of vocational guidance. Such experiences with religious work are more realistic than conversation or reading "about" church work could ever be. This is also related to recruitment. Such experiences may and often do lead to a decision to commit oneself to a career in the ministry or some other form of religious service. Again it emphasizes the unique opportunity of the pastor.

Vocational Counselor's Advantages

The vocational counselor has certain advantages over the pastor in counseling for church vocations. One of the primary advantages is that the vocational counselor has available in-

---

[4] Myers, *Principles and Techniques of Vocational Guidance* (New York: McGraw-Hill Book Company, 1941), p. 125. Used by permission.

formation about the young person that the pastor seldom has and if he doesn't have the information, he has the methods and techniques whereby it can be secured.

If he is related to an educational institution, he has the student's academic record which reveals not only his over-all grade average but the areas in which he has shown strength or weakness. It also indicates his extracurricular activities which give clues to his interests and leadership.

More important are his test scores on mental abilities, vocational aptitudes and interest, educational interest and achievement.

One criticism of the clergy by vocational counselors is that pastors are inclined to guess at such information. On occasion they tend to be sentimental and ignore the significance of such information. It is not enough because a boy is a good boy and his family is active in the church to say therefore that he would be a good preacher or medical missionary.

When a young person expresses an interest in medical missions, for example, certain definite and realistic questions have to be faced in the counselor's mind. Are his abilities such that he will finish high school with a grade average high enough to be accepted by college? What are his chances for completing a premedical course successfully in college? What are his chances of being accepted by a medical school? What are his chances of completing medical school? What are the probabilities that he will be accepted by the mission board as a candidate? Is his temperament such that he would be a good missionary doctor?

Such information can be secured most accurately by standardized tests. This is the area of the vocational counselor, not of the pastor.

The professional counselor has an advantage over the pastor in that he is often more psychologically oriented, with more training in counseling, and is thus better able to detect symptoms of other related or deep-seated emotional problems that may be present. Sometimes some of those related problems are of more ultimate significance than the vocational one.

It is also sometimes possible for the vocational counselor to be more objective. The pastor is often inclined to oversell the ministry to a young person, to make it a recruiting session when counseling and guidance is what is needed.

Sometimes the opposite is true. Some pastors have found the ministry so disheartening and their own experiences so disillusioning that they discourage young people from choosing one of the church vocations. This is the exception, however.

Some Common Problems of Counseling for Church Vocations

Many common problems arise in counseling for church vocations. Of course, the basic questions that are common to all vocational guidance are present. Is this what I really want to do? What does it involve? How will I spend my time? What are the advantages and disadvantages? How much training is required? Where is it secured? How much does it cost?

Often there are conflicting desires or alternating feelings— between the ministry and medicine, or ministry and teaching, or the ministry and law, as the case may be. These necessitate weighing one against the other, examining one's own aptitudes, motives, ambitions, and ideals.

Then there is the question of a choice of a college. What are the values of a church-related college over against a state university? What major should one take? What seminaries are available? These are important questions, for one's choice of a school influences his point of view, the quality of his preparation, his friendships, and the alumni group he will be associated with through the years.

Sometimes there is the problem of a choice within the field of church vocations. A young woman is trying to decide between church social work and missions, or between religious education and religious journalism. A young man may be struggling with the question, "Should I enter the pastorate or become a university pastor?" "Do I want to be a military chaplain or a missionary?" These are far-reaching questions. The counselee will live a different life and may live in different countries depending on the choice that he makes.

Sometimes the problem is of a more personal nature. The candidate for a church vocation may have a real feeling of inadequacy or unworthiness. He may wonder about his own personal qualifications. He may wonder about the reality of his call, or may have questions about religious doubt. He may feel called to the ministry but questions the call because many areas of religion are confusing or uncertain to him. He may feel sincerely called to religious work but have questions about the vitality of the church.

The list is endless. These are normal problems that all men face to some extent. With some one factor may seem more real, with some another. The pastor must be prepared to help think through such matters, whatever they may be.

Some Difficult Areas of Counseling for Church Vocations

Difficulty in reaching a decision is more a difference in degree than a difference in kind. Any of the problems mentioned above can become quite complex and may be very difficult.

Other problems are not infrequent and usually are quite difficult. Family opposition is one. This can be quite involved. It may and usually does require counseling with both the young person and his parents. At times there may be much misunderstanding coupled with strong feelings of hostility and guilt. A young person may be torn between two very real conflicting loyalties—an obligation to the ministry and devotion to his parents.

On the other hand, a family may have pressured a young person who is not qualified or interested in a church vocation into this choice. Others may enter out of a sense of duty, a sense of guilt.

Everyone who works in this area will have the experience of counseling and guiding a young person who simply does not have the ability to complete college and seminary. He will be consulted by those who do not have the emotional stability or who have some handicap which would make it inadvisable for them to consider the ministry. John Oliver Nelson speaks of alterable and unalterable handicaps. By alterable handicaps he means those things that can be overcome by "deliberate effort." By unalterable he means those things which cannot be changed and would greatly hamper professional competence. Among the alterable handicaps he lists the inability to get along with people, laziness, low academic standing, conceit, uncouth manner, hyper piousness of attitude, etc. Among the unalterable he includes grave physical disability, obvious emotional imbalance, serious speech defect, hereditary mental fault or dullness, complete "spinelessness," and weak constitution. Such a list serves to emphasize the seriousness and the difficulty of the problems encountered. Such a list can be dangerous. Who knows whether laziness and the inability to get along with people is alterable or not? Much depends on the motivation of the person and the skill and understanding of the counselor.

Low academic standing is alterable if the person has the ability and the motivation to improve; if he doesn't have, it is not. Serious speech defect may or may not be alterable. Speech therapists do some marvelous things. On the other hand, there are some areas of church vocations where a speech defect would not be too great a handicap.

Occasionally a pastor will be confronted with a person who is considering the ministry but who may have a very real moral or emotional problem. Often he is not seeking guidance but wants the pastor to endorse him or recommend him. Samuel Southard tells of a man who told his pastor that he had a call of God. "Everything is perfect between the Lord and me, and I'm ready to leave home and preach any time." When the pastor inquired about the "leaving home," he found that the man's marriage was practically on the rocks. Further investigation revealed the man had been "stepping out" on his wife who had threatened to leave. In this case Southard points out that the man saw the ministry as a refuge from guilt and social punishment.[5]

A young man in his late 20's approached a pastor about how he could get started in the ministry. His story included references to lights in the sky and other phenomena which he said indicated his call to preach. Further investigation disclosed a history of alcoholism, imprisonment, and psychotic behavior. Such a case illustrates the fact that in some cases motivation for entering religious service may actually be a sign of mental illness.

Some candidates for church vocations will need to be directed into other areas. Others by their own choice will conclude that church vocations is not the area in which they prefer to serve. This may be a wise decision but it does not relieve the pastor of responsibility. Every effort should be made to preserve the sense of commitment of these young people, to help them feel they still have a service to render. Every effort should be made to preserve the individual's self-respect, to help him feel his life is significant in the sight of God, that

---

[5] Southard, *op. cit.*, pp. 29-30. Used by permission.

he is respected as a person, that he has an important contribution to make through whatever occupation he may enter.

All counseling for church vocations should make the individual more effective as a layman if he does not enter the ministry. He should have a deeper appreciation of the ministry, a continuing commitment to the church, and a clearer understanding of his own qualifications and the way in which he can serve best.

An increasing problem is the older person who wants to enter the ministry. This trend has been so strong in recent years that a secular journal *The Saturday Evening Post* devoted a feature article to the subject. The author surveyed the various denominations and seminaries and reported that a Lutheran seminary had 87 candidates over 30 years of age, a Baptist seminary said 10% of their applications for admission were beyond 35, the Methodist Church in the previous year (1958) ordained 25 men who were over 45, the Episcopal Church in the last 7 years has ordained 127 men as deacons and 165 as priests who ranged from 36 to 72.[6]

There is every indication that this trend will continue. Men will leave the business world or professional life, or come out of the service and want to enter the ministry. This situation always presents related problems. There is the question of the man's wife and family. What is their attitude? What effect will it have on them? How will the loss of income or pension security affect them? What is the educational background of the candidate? Is he really qualified for college and seminary? Does he realize the meaning of long years of study? Is his motivation strong enough to carry him through the attendant discouragements, the questioning of friends? Is he really motivated to enter the ministry or is he running away from the discouragements of the business world?

[6] Cf. Spence: "Parsons Come Lately," *Saturday Evening Post*, August 29, 1959.

Some can and will make the change from the business world to the ministry. Others won't. Those who don't should still be led to see that they have a contribution to make, that any worthwhile work can become a Christian vocation. Some can make a ministry of their present job and all should serve the church more effectively as laymen, whether or not they enter the ministry professionally.

Principles of Counseling for Church Vocations

Certain principles should guide the pastor in counseling for church vocations:

(1) He should maintain a balance between recruitment and guidance. The pastor is expected to promote the ministry (by this we mean all church vocations). This must be done.

The shortage of qualified religious leaders at the present time is cause for due alarm. Between 1940 and 1950 the population increased by 19,000,000. Every city has vast new areas of housing developments; new shopping centers appear almost overnight. To meet these demands of a growing population and new neighborhoods many new churches have been established and all of them require pastors.

The trend toward a multiple ministry has influenced all denominations. Churches that 10 or 20 years ago were served by one man now may have several pastors, religious educators, youth workers on their staff. Not only local churches but councils of churches and state and national departments of all denominations have been increasing their staffs, most of which are drawn from local churches. Another new and growing development is the chaplaincy movement in institutions such as hospitals, mental hospitals, reformatories, and correctional institutions. Ever since World War II the military services have used large groups of men in the chaplaincy. A fairly recent development has been the ministry to students, the university chaplain, the denominational pastor.

While the demands have increased, the competition has also increased. Science and industry have maintained an intense recruiting program, the competition for the best minds of the country has been intensified due to the international situation and the cold war. While ministerial salaries have increased, they have not kept pace with those in some of these other areas.

The result has been that many religious leaders view the situation with alarm and have launched national programs to encourage pastors to intensify their efforts to secure a ministry. Such programs are needed; but this fact does not mean that every young person ought to enter the ministry. It does not mean that anyone should be pressured into such a decision.

Recruitment and guidance are not in opposition but are partners. Recruitment needs guidance. The real recruitment problem is not one of numbers. It is one of quality. It is a question of securing those who are competent and qualified for the task. This is always a guidance approach. Recruitment can create problems for guidance. Real difficulties have resulted when an emotionalized program of recruitment has enlisted one who is not qualified for the ministry. Recruitment is only the first step in a program of guidance and care. It is not enough to recruit a young person and then leave him to shift for himself. One reason there have been so many lost who once indicated an interest in the ministry is that young people were recruited but were left without a program to help them face their problems, to guide them through the total experience from interest to commitment, to training, to placement.

The pastor must recognize the need of both and the value of both.

(2) Counseling for church vocations should be done against

a background of a Christian philosophy for all worthy vocations. This is seen as a part of a total commitment. All men are called to Christian service. All men who are Christians are called to service in and for the church. Some are called to serve the church in a full-time professional way, some as laymen. The church is one way to serve God and one's fellow men—not the only way. Any calling that ministers to human needs is a Christian calling. There are many forms of full-time Christian service. The teacher, the doctor, the statesman, the housewife may all be rendering full-time Christian service.

Such a philosophy saves us from any false distinction between the sacred and the secular. It makes all life sacred. It avoids any temptation to self-righteousness or any implication that others are less Christian. It paves the way for future guidance of the young person who finds that the church is not the area where he can render the greatest service. He still can preserve his sense of commitment and need not feel any sense of unworthiness. It also emphasizes the tremendous significance of this whole task. It is more than finding a job. It is the process of searching to find God's will for a life. It is the manner in which one invests his time, his talents, himself.

(3) Counseling for church vocations should be seen in terms of its relationship to all other areas of experience. Counseling for church vocations is a part of a pastor's total counseling ministry. Here is a young man who wants to discuss the ministry. In the course of his conversation he says, "Now about my girl, she isn't too interested in the church." or another says, "I have often thought of the ministry but I feel so unworthy," or another says, "Missions really appeals to me but I have too many doubts of my own to try to help others."

The first focuses on a premarital situation, the second on the emotional feelings of unworthiness and guilt, and the third on religious doubt.

One who counsels on church vocations may find himself in any area of experience.

(4) All principles of good counseling and mental hygiene should be employed. This is not the place to discuss the techniques of counseling or the principles of mental hygiene. That has been done in many other volumes. But the counselor should keep in mind all of these factors; he will listen more than he talks, he recognizes that the young person's feelings are important, and so forth.

(5) Counseling for church vocations is a process that takes time. This fact is as true of guidance for church vocations as it is of any other. In fact, in some ways it may be more so because there is often more emotional involvement. It is a matter preachers are sometimes likely to forget. A young person comes with a question about entering the ministry. Many pastors feel that all the questions must be answered and his commitment completed in one interview. Counseling for church vocations is not an interview. One study of 700 ministers found that they averaged three years from the time they first thought about entering the ministry until they made their final decision. It also found that those who took the longest time in reaching the decision tended to be more likely to persist in the decision. There obviously are exceptions but such figures show that the minister's task is to act as counselor, guide, and friend throughout this process be it one year or five.

(6) The counselor for church vocations must utilize all resources available. This is the answer to the limitation mentioned earlier about test information, school records, and such data. The pastor can usually secure such information if he wishes. He should not guess at such matters as mental ability. If he is in doubt about whether or not a young person can do college and seminary work, he calls upon people trained to give the tests that provide him with such information. In some

cases where real emotional problems require counseling or therapy deeper than he can give, he utilizes the services of a psychiatrist or psychologist. If the candidate has a speech defect he utilizes a speech therapist, and so forth and so on.

Here as in all counseling he never attempts to do what someone else can do better. At the same time, he maintains contact as a pastor whatever sources of referral he uses.

(7) The decision of vocation is always the individual's. It is as true of counseling for church vocations as it is of any other that good vocational guidance is not telling another person what to do. Rather it is helping him gain such insights into his own personality and such an understanding of the field of church vocations that he can make a decision that is really his own.

This is a real temptation for the pastor. The need is so great, the shortage of ministers is so acute, the satisfaction of being able to say so many have entered the ministry under his leadership is so great that it is easy for a pastor to exert undue pressure or push for too early a decision.

The basic principle, however, remains the same. The pastor must respect the integrity of the individual. It is *his* decision and not the pastor's. This is the only decision that can be mature and permanent.

(8) The pastor should keep in mind two over-all objectives —the self-fulfillment of the individual, and the future of the church and the Christian cause. We do not claim that counseling on church vocations is the kind of problem that occurs frequently, although in some churches, especially in a university town, it may be. It may be that it occurs only once in every few years but when it does, it is a significant moment for the future of the candidate and for the future of the church.

VIII

THE MINISTER AND SPECIAL AREAS

OF

VOCATIONAL GUIDANCE

RETIREMENT AND THE OLDER WORKER

Every year shows an increase in the percentage of those who reach the age that government and industry consider retirement age. All indications are that this will continue to increase. This is one of the social phenomena of our times.

The United States Department of Health, Education and Welfare, in a publication entitled *"Aging—a Community Responsibility and Opportunity,"* states that since 1900 our total population has doubled, while the number of persons 65 years of age and over has quadrupled. Since 1930 the total population has increased by 30%, but the number of persons over 65 has increased by 100%. At the present time they say that there are more than 14,000,000 such persons in our communities and they estimate that by 1975 the number will be more than 21,000,000.

While the percentage of older persons has increased, employment opportunities have decreased. The Social Security Act of 1935 set 65 as the age for retirement. Some industries and professions have made it even lower. Some people are ready for retirement and welcome it at this age; others find it very difficult.

The shift from a rural to an urban society has eliminated many opportunities for activity for older persons. In a previous generation older persons could continue to be active on the farm, in a garden, or in household crafts and activities. Most of these are things of the past.

One of the most acute problems of older persons is the matter of employment. Some authorities feel that this is the major problem. The National Committee on Aging says, "For the vast majority, the chance to work—to have useful employment so long as health and strength permit—is the key to a happy and unfrustrated old age. It is the factor around which most other factors in this problem of the aging tend to revolve."[1]

Even though an early retirement has many attractions, it has been discovered that it is not good for many people and may not be good for society.

Older people have nowhere to go with their problems except to their pastors. Here, as with his young people, the pastor's counseling on vocational matters is part and parcel of his total ministry to the person. If he is to help them, his first task is to understand them and the nature of their problems. In this study we are limiting ourselves to the vocational area.

The older worker's problem, as his vocational opportunities are cut down or as he comes to the point of retirement, is characterized by loss—a loss of income, a loss of status and prestige, and often a loss of meaning and purpose.

The loss of income can be a very real problem. This influences many other areas of life. It limits the amount and quality of medical care that is available; it may affect housing;

[1] "Aging—a Community Problem," Washington, D.C., Committee on Aging and Geriatrics, p. 5.

it increases worry about the future. It also has many psychological and emotional accompaniments. For example, a woman had always given generously to her church. When retirement forced her to cut her pledge, she refused to attend, saying, "I will not go when I can't hold up my share."

In our culture income is not only a means of securing the necessities of life; it is a symbol of success and prestige. This the older worker does not have. Status and prestige, however, are determined not only by money; they are matters of position and responsibility. Many people get a large portion of their sense of worth and self-respect from the work they do. When the older worker finds himself replaced by a younger man and assigned to less important tasks, or when retirement eliminates vocational responsibilities entirely, he suffers a great sense of loss. He has been accustomed to a busy, active life; others have looked to him for advice and for the service he was able to render. Now this is gone.

This is, at root, a spiritual problem. Life has to have meaning. A man's work is one of the primary factors that give life meaning; without it, he loses a sense of purpose and meaning and value.

With retirement the former worker must learn a new role. Instead of going to the office or the shop, he remains at home. His wife continues her job as housewife, but his role has changed. It means long hours of idleness for him, a changing of his concept of himself, and, to a large extent, a change in his way of life.

This is a problem society must face. If the principle is true that older people can be happy and well-adjusted only when they are busy, and if society deprives them of the work which gives both financial security and a sense of worth, then society is obligated to find some form of assistance—financial and otherwise. It must find some means whereby these people feel that they have a useful and significant place in society.

Those who have studied the problem point out that many older persons can be productive; that their experience and training are valuable; and that society is suffering a great loss by the forced idleness and inactivity of people who are both capable and desirous of working.

This has economic implications for all of society. Some estimates indicate that if present trends continue and unless some plan for the employment of older persons is created in the future, every person under the age of 65 will be supporting someone past the age of 65.[2]

This is a concern of the pastor because he is a part of the community and, as such, he is interested in all social issues that have to do with the welfare of people. More than this, he is concerned because these are his people and they bring him all kinds of problems. This is one of their real problems and influences and affects all the other problems. The pastor is concerned because he is interested in the total well-being of his people—economically, emotionally, and spiritually.

Certain principles guide those who work with retired persons:

(1.) Each one is different. Retirement for one worker is a welcome relief; for another it is something dreaded and to be avoided. There are no stereotypes. Each must be seen in his own light.

(2.) Many older persons do want to work. Many want and need useful activity that will keep them busy. They do not want to be dependent. Some who are eligible for old-age assistance prefer to go on working instead.

(3.) Many of them *can* work. It is not a question of our

[2] Cf. Jeanne Gilbert, *Understanding Old Age* (New York, Ronald Press, 1952), p. 168.

being charitable to them. On the contrary, many employers have found that they can do a good job. Gilbert points out,

On the whole, the older employee is more stable, loyal, conscientious, and devoted to his job. Because of his long experience in a job, he often shows better judgment, wisdom, and strategy in his work. . . . It has been found that . . . there is less turnover, absenteeism, breakage and spoilage of material, fewer accidents, and fewer outside distractions, than found in younger employees.[3]

(4.) Sometimes the problem of the older worker is not his ability to do the work but his relationships with other employees. Some employers claim that older workers are difficult to get along with, are bossy and cantankerous, intolerant of new methods, and careless about their appearance. These criticisms are true of some older persons. This accounts, in part, for some of the prejudice against employing or keeping them on the job. One who works with older people may need to deal gently and diplomatically with such habits and attitudes.

(5.) Those who work with older persons agree that a tapering-off period is better than an abrupt change, or the cessation of all work altogether. Sometimes this can be accomplished by a transfer to another type of work that does not make the same physical demands.

(6.) A retired person may start a small business of his own. When the business is successful, it has many advantages. It provides income, occupies time and attention, and gives a sense of usefulness and value. In some instances it has permitted men to capitalize on hobbies or to pursue activities that have interested them for years. In other cases, men have been overly ambitious and have made serious mistakes and lost all of their savings. This leads only to frustration and disap-

[3] *Ibid.*, pp. 169f. Used by permission.

pointment. Starting a business is a place where the older person needs guidance and help. This may or may not be the pastor's task. This would depend upon his own experience and background. The fact that he may be the only one to whom the older person talks about his plans, the fact that he has the man's confidence means that he does have the responsibility to suggest that the older person secure the guidance of those whose judgment would be helpful before he invests much money or launches a program that is very extensive.

Any such venture should include a consideration of the worker's background and experience, his general health and strength. It should consider the potential demand for the service, the competitive factors in the field, the requirements in the way of capital that will be necessary. In general, it is not advisable for such a project to demand long hours or too large a financial investment.[4]

(7.) Many people can do odd jobs which may or may not be a source of income. The pastor and the church can often be a real help in securing them. A retired carpenter spent much of his time tinkering around the church, repairing furniture, fixing doors, making all sorts of improvements that had been needed for years. This was of actual value to the church and a genuine benefit to him. A retired minister voluntarily became a church caller, visiting indifferent and prospective members and became a big help to the pastor.

Not all work of this kind is confined to the church; retired persons can render a real contribution to social agencies as well. A retired barber cut the hair of children in an institution; a cabinet maker repaired toys for children; an artist gave free art lessons to any who wished them. The organization of gray ladies in hospitals is a form of service that is of great benefit to the hospital and also to those who serve.

[4] The Department of Commerce has available bulletins on many small enterprises.

This form of vocational guidance is one that deserves increased attention and study.

(8.) Vocational counseling with the elderly requires a great deal of time. In the first place, it is usually a part of other problems that the older person wants to discuss, and the pastor, by virtue of his interest in the person, is interested in all areas of the person's need. It requires time because there are no established outlets for the services of such a person. It may require considerable searching and exploration by both pastor and older person before they find the specific area, industry, job, or part-time job that matches the interests, strength, and experience of the prospective worker. It requires a longer time for older persons to tell their story, to express their feelings, and discuss their problems.

(9.) The pastor's vocational counseling with retired and older persons is usually a part of his total pastoral care program. By this we mean that most of it grows out of other pastoral contacts. Only occasionally will an older person make an appointment to discuss a job or to work out plans for some part-time work. Rather, the pastor usually learns about this need when he calls in the home just to express his interest about a man's retirement; or he may make a routine pastoral call (which we hope he does with all his older church members) and, as a part of the conversation, hear the older person express his feelings of uselessness, his financial concerns, his desire to work, his plan for starting a small business, or whatever the case may be. Then the pastor is in a position to offer counsel and guidance and help, and to suggest others who could help. The pastor who calls regularly in the homes of his older parishioners, who sees them at all times, in illness, and so forth, will be the one who has the opportunity to help with this very real problem.

THE RETARDED AND THE GIFTED

Intelligence is an important factor that must be considered in both vocational choice and adjustment. Those whose mental abilities are very much above or very much below the average have their own unique vocational problems as a result of their intellectual differences. This is an area that has received very little attention in the literature on vocational guidance and practically none in the literature on pastoral counseling.

The Retarded

The retarded child has many problems. One is his vocational limitations and the problem this creates in vocational choice and adjustment. This group includes not only the severely retarded who are in institutions or who are kept at home and not allowed to attend school. It includes the slow learners whose intellectual level is such that they are placed in a special or ungraded class at school, or who, in schools where no provision is made for special training, experience repeated failure or are moved from one grade to the next without grasping the material.

Many of these young people drop out of school at an early age, seldom going beyond that made compulsory by school law. They thus separate themselves from the guidance services of the school. They have no one to whom to turn for help with their personal and vocational problems. If their families are church-related, they may go to the pastor for help. More frequently the parents may seek help first, wondering what they should do.

Employment for these young people has values beyond the economic needs of an income, although this can be very real, especially in a large family in which the family income may be relatively low. However, unemployment means idleness, inactivity which can lead to delinquency and immorality. When a young person reaches the age at which others are self-supporting or partially so, he feels a loss of status and a sense of worthlessness and inadequacy if he is doing nothing.

Many of these young persons can work. They can be wholly or partially self-supporting if they can find people who are patient enough to help them to develop the aptitudes by which they can secure and maintain a position, develop the simple skills that are needed, and locate the places where these skills can be used.

Here, as everywhere in such work, there are certain principles that should guide anyone working with the retarded:

(1.) First of all, it is necessary to be sure he is retarded. This is not an area in which one should guess. Whether the problem is vocational or academic, the one who is working with the retarded should be sure that he has a thorough and accurate evaluation by those competent to administer the necessary tests and to make such an evaluation.

There have been enough examples of young people listed as retarded who actually had average or superior ability to make the counselor cautious. Apparent retardation was due to emotional causes or physical handicaps, like inadequate sight or hearing.

Here, for example, is a young man who was thought to be so retarded that he was being considered for an institution for the retarded. Then it was discovered that he is hard of hearing. He had never heard his parents, his teachers, or anyone else who talked to him. No one knew that he was hard of hearing. Vocational guidance could do him a grave injustice if it proceeded on the basis of his being retarded. What he really needs is a hearing aid, personal counseling to work through some of his emotional problems, and then vocational guidance that takes into account both his handicap and his average abilities which could enable him to maintain a responsible position.

The Associated Press carried a story which received nation-wide publicity of a man who spent his entire youth and much of his adult life in a home for the retarded. Then it was discovered that he had above-average intelligence and was quite capable of supporting himself. Obviously, such a person needs extensive counseling to make the adjustment from a life in an institution to that of self-supporting citizenship in society. Someone made a mistake. He was dealt with as being a retarded person when obviously, he was not.

It should also be pointed out that there is a decided difference between being mentally retarded and educationally retarded. A person may be educationally retarded because of a language handicap, a lack of motivation, or the fact that his family has moved often. A person who is educationally retarded may or may not be mentally retarded.

(2.) Vocational choice for the retarded must be within the range of his mental abilities. Any attempt to carry on a job that requires more intellectual capacity than the person possesses only leads to frustration and failure.

This creates problems of its own. The number of such jobs that are available is limited in number. The retarded youth often has ambitions for positions beyond his abilities. This is accentuated by the fact that many industries and professions are carrying on extensive recruiting programs, urging all young people to take advantage of the great opportunities that are available. It is true that the opportunities are there—but only for those who have the capacity to secure the training and to do the task.

The retarded youth has further pressures in that many of his friends and classmates are making decisions for professional training and are entering highly skilled trades. Naturally he would like to join them. His parents may not realize his limitations and they, too, may push him into college experiences or vocational positions in which he is bound to fail.

(3.) Vocational guidance with the retarded should, if possible, include the parents and the rest of the family. Sometimes parents have prevented a young person from securing employment that would bring both income and satisfaction because they wanted him in a position of more prestige and status.

(4.) Vocational guidance with the retarded should be a part of a counseling program that includes other matters of personal and social adjustment. Only rarely is a problem with a retarded youth strictly a vocational problem. Those who have worked extensively with the retarded in this field find that a good share of their time is spent in dealing with personality problems, work habits, social adjustment, and so forth. This is an area in which the pastor should have a distinct contribution.

(5.) The church must emphasize the sacredness of all honest work. Status and prestige are extremely important in our culture. This is another of the problems of the retarded. The kind of work that he can do has little status or prestige. He never experiences the sense of satisfaction that others achieve because of the positions that they hold.

The church needs to keep before them, and before all men for that matter, the sacredness of all honest effort. The pastor can do this better than any one else since it is more a matter of theology than one of economics. If a man has two talents and has done his best, he is entitled to the same reward as the man with five. "Well done, thou good and faithful servant." This is all that is asked of anyone.

(6.) The pastor should be familiar with all resources that help the retarded in vocational matters. He is not a specialist in vocational guidance or in the field of the retarded. When a retarded youth or a member of his family comes to the pastor for help, one of his best contributions may be to get him to the people who can render the most effective service. The department of special education of the public school has probably already had experience with the young person. It knows from observation and from psychological test scores what can be expected of him academically and vocationally. Before proceeding to any serious counseling or guidance, the pastor should consult with this resource.

Since 1943 the mentally retarded have been eligible for both guidance and training through the office of vocational rehabilitation.

Many communities have associations for retarded children, some with full-time executives, who can give information about employers who will use retarded persons. Some of these associations maintain sheltered workshops where a person can be at least partially self-supporting. This, if doing nothing more than giving him an opportunity to use his time, has some value.

(7.) It should be remembered that many of the retarded can work. The experience of such groups as those mentioned above has proved that many retarded persons, hitherto doomed to uselessness and idleness, can earn either all or part of their income and thus become self-respecting, tax-paying citizens. It is estimated that a large percentage of persons with IQ's between 50 and 70 could be earning their own living if they had some guidance and training.

It is true that their jobs must be routine and unskilled and seemingly monotonous, but what is monotonous to the average or gifted may be quite creative and satisfying to the retarded. In fact, in some areas, the retarded may be better qualified than their more gifted neighbors. In routine work that requires simple directions they may be more efficient and better workers than those with more ability. In some cases they may be less accident prone. As one punch-press operator of low mentality said, "It's only them that thinks that lose their fingers."[5]

(8.) Work with the retarded takes great patience and time and understanding. These people cannot always make decisions; they do not come to insights as the gifted do. They, too, need to express their feelings; they need someone who understands their frustrations. In vocational matters they may need someone who serves as a guide and an instructor. As stated above, experience shows that they can produce results in the vocational field, but they need help.

The Gifted

Vocational guidance of the gifted is important because these people have much to contribute and because they are persons. As persons, it is important that they find that vocation in which they will feel the greatest satisfaction and sense of fulfillment. They can be just as unhappy in the wrong vocation as the retarded or those with average intelligence—more so, perhaps.

The fact remains that the gifted have a great potential for good or ill. Those who work with them must be aware of this fact. In the main, it is going to be the gifted who are in positions of leadership and influence and therefore it is important for all of society that they find their places in positions where they can make the greatest contributions. It is important to help the retarded find a place because of their own needs but they are not going to have the influence on society or make the contribution the gifted can make.

[5] James Gillespie, *Free Expression in Industry* (London: Pilot Press, Ltd. 1948), p. 41.

If a pastor has even one boy in his youth group who has great intellectual or leadership ability, he has a tremendous responsibility. This one boy, if he is properly challenged and guided, may become a tremendous influence for good in the field of medicine, education, religion, or statesmanship.

The vocational problems of the gifted are almost the reverse of those of the retarded:

(1.) With the retarded the problem is the limitation of the number of things that he can do; with the gifted it is the fact that there are so many things that he can do and can do well that it is a problem of selecting one out of many and saying, "This is the thing I would rather do than anything else."

Gifted children, almost as a pattern, have a wide range of interests. There are so many things they enjoy and in which they could succeed that it is sometimes difficult to select one and make preparation for it.

(2.) The vocational choice of the gifted should not be hurried. The retarded needed vocational training early. They are not going to stay in school anyway. With the gifted the opposite is true. A definite decision should be deferred until they have had a full chance to explore all of their interests and all possibilities. The fact that more than half of the college students in our universities change their majors in the course of their education indicates how these interests shift and change.

(3.) With the retarded the problem is to find a job that does not demand more ability than he has, otherwise he will meet only frustration. With the gifted person the problem is to find a job that challenges his capacities or he will meet only frustration.

One of the tragic things in our country is the fact that there are many who are capable of a college education and of a position that demands real creative mental abilities but who find themselves sidetracked into dead-end monotonous jobs. The result is dissatisfaction on the part of the individual and a tragic loss to society.

(4.) Parents need to be included in the vocational guidance of the gifted, too. With the retarded they are often not aware of their child's limitations. With the gifted they may not be aware of his possibilities. This is primarily true in the lower socioeconomic groups in which the parents have not had a background of college and training and may not see its value for their children; in fact, they may openly oppose it.

Here, for example, is a young man whose high school record and his mental and aptitude test scores would indicate that he has great potential for academic success and, perhaps, for success in one of the professions. However, his father is a plumber who quit school at the end of the eighth grade. He thinks the boy ought to go out and get to work. After all, the father tells the boy, he makes more at his plumbing than the college professors do. In this case, he is right. But he fails to sense at all the boy's potentialities or his emotional needs for self-fulfillment.

(5.) The retarded must be made aware of the sacredness of all honest work. The gifted, however, must be made aware of the sacredness of his own responsibility. This must be done carefully and cautiously so that the gifted one does not become an intellectual snob; rather, it should make him humble. The New Testament says, "Every one to whom much is given, of him will much be required." (Luke 12:48b.)

(6.) The counseling approach, too, will be different. The counselor needs to be directive with the retarded; he should be very permissive with the gifted. The counselor creates the atmosphere in which the counselee thinks clearly, free from emotion, surveying all possibilities, weighing all factors—then he makes his own decision.

THE HANDICAPPED

The word "handicap" has a variety of meanings. The dictionary refers to it as "any disadvantage that renders success more difficult." Such disadvantages have a vast range of both difficulty and variety. They apply to everyone to some extent. This study, however, is concerned primarily with physical handicaps, their effect on vocational success and adjustment, and the role of the minister if any, in helping in this area.

Almost every community, every congregation has its share of handicapped persons. Some have been handicapped since birth; others have not. With some the handicap is obvious; with others it cannot be seen or recognized. The United States Office of Education estimates that at least 12% of all school children are handicapped to some degree. Among adults the percentage may be even larger. It includes those who have been handicapped by industrial accidents and illness, and, of course, the many veterans who are handicapped as a result of war.

Historically speaking, the plight of the handicapped has not been a pleasant one. In ancient times these people were subject to ridicule and were commonly neglected and often persecuted and mistreated.

Even among the enlightened Greeks exposure and infanticide were accepted for weak and deformed infants. Such famous men as Aristotle, Plato, and Seneca accepted and defended such practices. No one wanted to be bothered with a handicapped child.

With the coming of the Christian era, a new spirit of compassion came into the world. The Christian religion brought a message of love in which the strong bore the burdens of the weak and men were taught that they had a responsibility of rendering a service to others, especially to the needy and the unfortunate.

For centuries it was primarily the church that showed any concern. The first institutions for the deaf and the handicapped were established by the church. Their activities were originally acts of charity providing for the physical needs of the afflicted.

In the nineteenth century medical science became interested but placed its emphasis mainly on physical care. In the twentieth century programs of special education were developed. Men in the field of educational psychology began to publish studies of the exceptional child. Special equipment was devised, classes were formed, and teachers received training in special educational methods and procedures.

The most recent development is a program of vocational training and rehabilitation. Vocational rehabilitation has as its purpose to help the person attain his maximum capacity physically, emotionally, and vocationally so that he can become an independent, self-supporting adult. In the case of the child, this means securing the needed education and training. In the case of an adult, it may mean retraining and restoring the desire to work. In every case it involves training, counseling, and placement.

This field has developed its own group of specialists, trained in specific skills and techniques which are necessary for vocational rehabilitation. The results, in a comparatively brief period of time, are most encouraging. Great progress can be cited both in individual cases and in some very significant statistics.

Physical handicaps are of many varieties. They include those who are visually handicapped, deaf and hard of hearing, orthopedically handicapped, speech handicapped, spastic, and many others. In a sense those who are too tall or too short, too small or too large may be handicapped for some positions. The person with a birthmark or some disfigurement is handicapped if his or her ambitions lie in certain areas.

Vocationally speaking it is the degree of the handicap that is important. Three gradations may be noted although at times it is difficult to determine where one leaves off and the next begins.

(1.) First and most frequent are the minor handicaps. Children thus afflicted are educated in the regular classroom of the public school. As adults, they work at many different types of jobs; they get about in the community; they may be active in church. Their handicaps may create some very real problems emotionally, but they do not greatly impair them vocationally.

(2.) Those who have more serious handicaps may require the care of a specialist. In school they may need special equipment, such as hearing aids, crutches, braces, or special classes, special training, such as Braille, speech therapy, and so forth. Vocationally they need guidance to find the area in which they can work and preparation and training to fit them for it.

(3.) The third group includes the severely handicapped who can be only partially self-supporting or who may not be able to work at all. They are the homebound and those who are in hospitals and institutions for the handicapped.

The pastor is concerned about all of these persons. He is concerned as a pastor about their total welfare—their attitudes, their feelings, their spiritual growth and adjustment as well as their vocational plans and adjustments. His concern and approach are quite different from that of the representative of the office of vocational rehabilitation; yet, if the pastor does his job well, he may make a real contribution to the person's vocational rehabilitation.

Two basic factors will influence the direction of the guidance: (1) the disability itself: the limitation it places on the individual, the treatment and the training that it requires; and (2) the individual's personal reaction to it: What does it mean to him? What are his feelings about it?

In working with the vocational problems of the handicapped certain principles should guide the pastor:

(1.) Not all handicapped persons want or need help. Many are self-reliant, self-supporting, well-adjusted persons. The pastor should not read problems into situations where no problem exists.

(2.) Handicapped persons are individuals. They should not be stereotyped as a group. Some handicapped persons are overly sensitive, withdrawn, and inhibited. Some become cynical and discouraged. Also, some nonhandicapped persons are overly sensitive and withdrawn. Not all handicapped persons are overly sensitive or withdrawn. In other words, there is no psychology of the handicapped as such, therefore each individual must be treated as a person in his own right.

(3.) Two paradoxical thoughts should always be kept in mind in dealing with the handicapped: (a) the fact that they are different, and (b) the fact that they are essentially the same as everyone else. Both facts are important. The limitations are real; they may affect what the person can and cannot do. The handicaps may demand special training and preparation. At the same time, it should always be remembered that these persons are essentially the same as everyone else. The visually handicapped person is one who cannot see, the hard of hearing is a person who cannot hear—both desire love, attention, a sense of achievement and accomplishment. Their feelings are the same as everyone else's.

(4.) Emphasis should always be on what the subject *can* do, not on what he *cannot* do. It is what a person *can* do that is important. A man may be handicapped in one area but very effective in another. Though a person may have definite limitations in some areas, he also has areas of vocational usefulness and productivity. Because a person is in a wheel chair does not mean that he cannot use his hands or his mind.

Psychologically the emphasis should be on what he *can* do. Practical plans for selection, training, and placement must be in terms of the areas in which he can succeed.

(5.) Every effort should be made to help these persons accept responsibilities. There is a tendency to pity them, to feel sorry for them. Some may develop attitudes of resignation and feel that they ought to be waited upon. They must be helped to feel that they have a part to play, that they have a contribution to make. Both self-acceptance and self-reliance are goals toward which to work; one depends upon the other.

(6.) The pastor should know the resources that are available for specialized help. He should be familiar with the groups and agencies that render assistance to the handicapped, such as the Office of Vocational Rehabilitation, Goodwill Industries, Employment Service, Department of the Blind, Special Education, the Veterans' Administration, and so forth. There are many persons who have specialized training for working with the handicapped: speech therapists, vocational rehabilitation counselors, occupational therapists, social workers who can make use of special techniques and equipment to help handicapped persons find their vocations and secure training in them.

It is not the pastor's place to be trained in such techniques. It is his responsibility to know that they exist. Very often the handicapped person and his family do not know that such organizations exist or are hesitant about asking for such help.

The pastor's responsibility is to work with such specialists in a co-operative or team approach.

(7.) The pastor should be aware that tremendous strides

have been made. The Office of Vocational Rehabilitation reports that more than 7,000,00 people with physical impairments are now employed.

Another report from this same office, issued in 1957, said that in fourteen years of operation of the State-Federal program 778,000 handicapped men and women had been rehabilitated by state vocational rehabilitation agencies. In 1956, 66,000 handicapped persons, the majority of whom had no earnings at all, were enabled to become self-supporting. In 1957, 71,607 were rehabilitated—an increase of 8% over the previous year. Every indication is that the trend will continue.

Switzer and Rusk in their book, *Doing Something for the Disabled*, state, "Never before in human history have the opportunities for restoration of the disabled been so promising. Today we can approach with confidence many disabling conditions which, even as recently as twenty years ago, were generally accepted as hopeless."

They cite an illustration of 400 persons living in a county home for the poor, all of whom were considered permanent wards of the public. After a modest program of vocational rehabilitation 25% returned to jobs, 25% returned home and were able to care for themselves, 25% were able to move about within the institution and benefited from a better adjustment, and 25% received no observable benefit.[6]

(8.) Experiences with vocational rehabilitation have proved that handicapped workers are good workers. They are careful, capable, reliable, and regular. Their work records compare favorably with those of nonhandicapped workers. Their absenteeism record is as good as that of the nonhandicapped. Their safety record is as good or better than average. For minor

---

[6] Switzer and Rusk, Public Affairs Pamphlet No. 197. *Doing Something for the Disabled*, pp. 28 and 21. May be secured from the Public Affairs Committee, 22 East 38th Street, New York 16, N. Y. 25 cents.

156   THE PASTOR AND VOCATIONAL COUNSELING

injuries it is about the same. For major injuries it is less than average. Their production rate is as good as or better than that of the nonhandicapped.

Furthermore, it has been found that this is true in almost every area of vocational life. Again, it is the same principle. Although a person may be handicapped in one area, he is not in another.

(9.) The personal or emotional factors are as real as the technical matters of training and equipment. This is why the pastor has an important part to play. Vocational development is closely related to a worker's development of a self-concept. With the handicapped this is particularly important because he must develop a realistic self-concept if he is to find satisfaction either vocationally or personally.

Often the determining factor is not the medical treatment, not special equipment or the availability of a program of training; it is the ability or will to persist in the efforts. This is especially true in such areas as speech therapy, for example. This is a matter of motivation; it is a question of whether or not the subject feels it is worthwhile. This again is an area in which the pastor has a contribution.

(10.) Families are usually involved. They, too, need guidance and help for their own needs and in order that they can be more helpful to the handicapped. Not infrequently these family involvements may complicate or impede vocational counseling and training.

In one group of 69 disabled welfare recipients, it was found that 120 other persons—wives, children, parents, and so forth—were personally involved in their problems and, to some extent, dependent upon them.[7]

The specialist in vocational rehabilitation may work with the handicapped person in terms of his needs and his training,

[7] Ibid., p. 8.

but the pastor can be a great help by working with the whole family.

(11.) The handicapped have spiritual needs. The determining factor in their vocational rehabilitation may be the depth of their faith. It is through religion that they find fortitude, meaning, and purpose in life. This is the pastor's specialty.

In this country there are literally thousands—in fact, some authorities say there are millions—of disabled people who need and could benefit from specialized vocational help, who could be restored to vocational usefulness, to economic independence, and to a sense of self-reliance and self-respect, but who are not now receiving any help at all. It is estimated that some 250,000 persons are disabled each year from some cause or another but only about 60,000 are rehabilitated each year. Every effort should be made to assist them in securing the help they need. Many do not receive help because they do not know that the possibility exists. This is the pastor's task —to know what facilities are available and to aid the disabled in finding and accepting the help they need. At the same time many more people need to be recruited and trained for such work. Results thus far prove what can be done.

Someone has said that much of the great work of the world has been done by handicapped people. Milton was blind, as was George Mathieson, hymn writer and theologian. Beethoven and Rauschenbusch were deaf. Edison was considered stupid by his teachers when actually he couldn't hear. Virgil, and Charles Lamb had speech defects. Moses protested when he was called to a position of leadership because he was "slow of speech and slow of tongue." The list could be extended to much greater length. Such lives are inspirations, a demonstration of what can be done.

Helen Keller spoke for all the handicapped people when

she said, "My limitations never make me unhappy . . . I like to think that through my limitations God is working out some good purposes. My troubles have always been great adventures. They have brought me understanding friendship, and taught me how to serve the world."

OTHER GROUPS

Other persons sometimes come to the pastor for help with vocational problems—the ex-convict, the patient discharged from a mental hospital, the alcoholic, the transient who wants a job. Calls of this kind are usually infrequent but when they do come, they can be very difficult and complex. Here, for example, is a young man recently paroled from the state penitentiary who is referred to a pastor. In the course of the conversation he says, "I want to go straight but I can't. I must have money to live but I can't get a job. I know all the questions. They say, 'What is your name? Age? Previous place of employment?' When I say, 'The machine shop at the state penitentiary,' they say, 'Sorry, but we're full up now. Don't call us; we'll call you.' Or, I can lie about it and get the job but, sooner or later, they find out I did time, then they fire me. I've got to work but I can't get a job, so all I can do is steal."

A patient discharged from a state hospital may have a similar problem. One embarrassing experience or the fear of a repetition of this may cause him to give up and not attempt to find work at all.

An alcoholic has been working with the pastor for some time. He has lost two or three jobs and, at the present time, is out of work. He has heard of a good job which he wants and needs. In conversation with his pastor, he says, "I have a chance for just the job I've always wanted. I used your name for a reference. I hope you don't mind."

A transient drifts into a community and calls on the pastor. "I'm a member of your church in Indiana," he says. "I know you'll help me. If you'll just call up some of these men and recommend me, I know I can get a job."

These are different cases. Often the person's vocational needs may be one of the primary factors in his rehabilitation. Work in itself is one of the best forms of therapy. A good job means recognition; it provides status in the community; it gives a man a feeling of self-respect; and it provides the income so sorely needed by the person and his family.

The pastor knows all of this. He recognizes the person's need for a job, but he cannot always be sure of the motivation of the person who comes for help. The pastor also has a responsibility to the employer who may, on occasion, be a member of his church—or a personal friend.

There are no rules to follow in such cases but there are a few principles that should be kept in mind.

(1.) The pastor should secure as thorough a background of information about the applicant as possible. In the case of the ex-convict he would do well to get in touch with the prison chaplain and social service department so that he can find out something of the kind of man with whom he is dealing. In the case of the discharged mental patient, he could secure valuable information from the physician, the psychiatrist, or the psychiatric social worker.

(2.) To secure vocational help for such persons, it is necessary that the pastor know the attitudes of the employers. It does no good to recommend a man for a job if he will not be accepted. The attitude of the employer and other workers may be just as important as the nature of the work.

(3.) All such matters should be handled with strict honesty.

All details need not be revealed nor should confidences be violated. However, the pastor has an obligation to both parties, the employer and the employee. It does no good in securing a position for a man who is an ex-convict, for example, to cover up the fact, only to have it be discovered later and run the risk of having the man fired. One pastor who has had unusual success with alcoholics has an understanding with them when they use his name as a reference. He insists that he give this information to the prospective employer, along with the fact that the man is seeing him and is making an honest effort to overcome the habit. If the man refuses, then the pastor will not give his recommendation. If he consents, then both employer and employee start with an understanding of the situation.

(4.) The pastor, when confronted with such situations, should make use of the services of the agencies that exist just for such purposes. It is not the pastor's place to be an employment agency. The employment services usually know the employers who will employ ex-convicts on a full-time basis. The City Mission or Rescue Mission very commonly find part-time or brief employment for transients. Some mission workers know all the men in town who have just part-time jobs available. They can find a job for a transient in a matter of minutes when it might take a pastor all day and are usually more than willing to co-operate. The unemployed often do not know the resources that are available. The pastor's task is to make it possible for them to get to the ones who can give them definite practical help.

(5.) The pastor's chief responsibility is to function as a pastor. He deals with the whole person. He recognizes how important vocational opportunities and vocational adjustment are to these persons. He is aware of the resources of the community; then he continues his relationship as a pastor, providing the services and resources he is trained and qualified to give. Vocational help is important but these people also need personal and spiritual help. This is the pastor's opportunity and responsibility.

Appendixes

Appendix I

A Chronological Chart of the Development of the Vocational Guidance Movement

We are well aware that vocational guidance took place long before 1836. Also we know we have overlooked some events, perhaps of real significance. We have tried to list a few of the events that have contributed toward making it a movement.

1836 – Edward Hazen published *Panorama of Professions and Trades,* a forerunner of occupational information material.

1881 – Lysander Richards published *Vocaphy* in which he advocated a new profession to help persons find the right vocation. He envisioned a new profession like law or medicine. These persons were to work as counselors and be known as "vocaphers." He made no effort to follow it up, however.

1884 – President White of Cornell published *What Profession Shall I Choose and How Shall I Fit Myself for It?* There were several such books. They were information-centered. The concept of counseling and guidance was not included.

1888 – George Merrill tried an experiment in vocational education in San Francisco.

1894 – George A. Merrill instituted a program of vocational education at San Francisco. Vocational education was primary and a form of vocational guidance was secondary.

1902 – Edgar J. Helms established Goodwill Industries in Boston to provide training and employment for handicapped.

1905 – Binet presented his first intelligence scale. Many other tests were to follow. The mental testing movement, which made it possible to secure an objective measure of a person's abilities, offered a very helpful tool to the vocational counselor.

1905 – Frank Parsons became director of the Breadwinners' Institute in Boston.

1907 – Parsons gave a talk to a high school senior class on the choice of a vocation which led to many personal interviews.

1908 – First course for vocational counselors sponsored by the Educational Committee of the Boston Y.M.C.A.

1908 – Vocation Bureau of Boston was formed with Parsons as Director and Vocational Counselor. The first annual report used the term "vocational guidance" for the first time.

1908 – Parsons worked in a Y.M.C.A. program of vocational guidance. Other Y's across the country began to include programs of vocational guidance in their activities. This was especially true of Student Y's.

1909 – *Choosing a Vocation*, by Frank Parsons was published.

1909 – Appointment of a Committee on Vocational Advice by Boston School System.

1909 – National Committee for Mental Hygiene formed with Clifford Beers as executive secretary. The mental hygiene movement was to have a profound effect on vocational guidance.

1910 – The National Urban League established "to further the industrial advancement of the Negro" included vocational guidance of Negroes in its program.

1910 – School system of Boston began a study on need of vocational guidance.

1910 – First national conference on vocational guidance.

1911 – Publication of *Vocational Guidance News-Letter*.

1911 – The first educational vocational guidance survey was conducted by Stanford University. An indication of a new but growing movement to provide a counseling service in college and universities.

1911 – Publication of Meyer Bloomfield's book *The Vocational Guidance of Youth.*

1911 – Harvard offered first course in the training of those who would do vocational guidance.

1912 – A Placement Bureau was established in Roxbury (part of Boston).

1912 – Grand Rapids, Michigan, organized a Department of Vocational Guidance. Soon many other cities also announced such programs.

1912 – Organization of Employment Managers' Association. This marked the awareness of a new profession—the personnel worker in industry.

1913 – National Vocational Guidance Association formed.

1914 – Stenquist Construction Tests of Mechanical Ability. This soon followed by other aptitude tests in areas such as art, clerical ability, stenography, teaching, nursing, engineering, etc.

1915 – Publication of *Vocational Guidance Bulletin,* a national journal.

1915 – Truman Kelley prepared a doctor's thesis entitled *Educational Guidance.*

1915 – Seashore Measures of Musical Talent appeared. One of first aptitude tests.

1917 – Development of Army Alpha made available group tests of mental ability. Army Beta made tests available for illiterate and foreign born.

1918 – United States Employment Service made a Branch of the Department of Labor, primarily to help industry rather than workers.

1924 – National Vocational Guidance Association defined vocational guidance as "the giving of information, experience, and advice in regard to choosing an occupation, preparing for it, entering it, and progressing in it."

1924 – The *Vocational Guidance Bulletin* became the *Vocational Guidance Magazine*.

1925 – National Rehabilitation Association established to promote vocational guidance of handicapped.

1927 – Strong's Vocational Interest Inventory appeared after 19 years of research and investigation.

1932 – New York Council of Jewish Federations and Welfare Funds included a committee on vocational agencies in the Jewish field. B'nai B'rith Hillel Foundation carries on an extensive vocational guidance program.

1933 – *Vocational Guidance Magazine* changed name to *Occupations*.

1937 – National Vocational Guidance Association changed its definition from "giving advice" to "The process of assisting the individual to choose an occupation, prepare for it, etc."

1938 – Plans were made for the Occupational Information and Guidance Service in the Vocational Division of the U.S. Office of Education.

1939 – *Kuder Preference Record—Vocational.*

1939 – Publication of *Dictionary of Occupational Titles* by United States Employment Service listing 17,452 different jobs.

1939 – Reorganization bill was passed creating the Federal Security Agency which included United States Employment Service.

1942 – Carl Rogers published *Counseling and Psychotherapy*, a book which marked the beginning of interest in the non-directive, or client-centered, approach to counseling. This is an emphasis which has had a major influence in vocational guidance.

1946 – Publication by Carroll L. Shartle of a text, *Occupational Information*.

1948 – The First Assembly of the World Council of Churches gave attention to the problem of a Christian doctrine of work and vocation.

1949 – Revised edition of *Dictionary of Occupational Titles* published, containing descriptions of 22,028 jobs, which are known by an additional 17,995 titles, making a total of 40,023 defined titles.

1952 – American Personnel and Guidance Association formed amalgamating several groups.

1952 – Journal *Occupations* changed name to *The Personnel and Guidance Journal*.

1954 – The World Council of Churches meeting at Evanston included a section on work and vocation.

Appendix II

Quotations on the Theological Interpretation of Vocation

There is an increasing tendency among theologians to emphasize the theological implications of vocation and to develop a Christian doctrine of work. The following quotations are but a small sample of some thoughts in this field.

Emil Brunner
The problem of the meaning of work leads us right into the ultimate question of the meaning of life itself.

.   .   .   .   .   .

The attitude to work is ultimately a religious question.

.   .   .   .   .   .

If people take their Christian faith seriously, everyone knows that his specific function in society is served for the common good.[1]
World Council of Churches, Evanston Assembly 1954
Today many people are asking whether Christianity has any relevance to their daily work. They feel that there is a gulf between the Church and its worship and their workaday lives.

.   .   .   .   .   .

This gulf between the Church and the life of the world can be bridged by those who have a Christian view of work.[2]

Reuel L. Howe
A . . . *corrective to our attitude toward work is to see it as a part of God's work.* All work that contributes to the common good is

[1] Brunner, *Christianity and Civilisation* (New York: Charles Scribner's Sons, 1949), pp. 67, 66, 63. Used by permission of Charles Scribner's Sons and of James Nisbet & Company, Limited.
[2] The Evanston Report, p. 154.

171

God's. According to the Bible, God is known by His action in the actual every day business of living, of social relationships, and of current historical events. The worker, therefore, serves God by doing faithfully His work. By our work we participate in God's creation in many ways. The study and experimentation that opened up our knowledge of nuclear physics is an example of the creative powers God has given us. We might be tempted to think that the creativity shown in that discovery belonged only to the scientists who directly engaged in the study and experimentation. But all mankind, directly and indirectly, shared in the discovery. . . . The faithfulness of one man was just as important as that of others. For each by his faithfulness to his particular task was imitating Christ who was faithful in His task of saving the world. There are differences in tasks, but faithfulness is faithfulness, no matter what the task.

. . . .

This same truth was impressed upon me one beautiful day as I stood waiting for a streetcar, on the corner of a big, busy, dirty city. I noticed two street cleaners, one on each side of the street, moving slowly toward me as they brushed the dirt into piles along the gutters. One was doing his job well, the other wasn't. When the man on my side of the street came abreast of me, I commented on the neat job he was doing. He glanced at me in surprise. Then, looking back over his work, he said in his broken English, "She do looka good, huh?" Then, he pointed to the blue sky overhead and said, "God's world, she very beautiful. Me, I gotta go to work." With that he went on down the street sweeping into neat piles the refuse of a careless city.

There went a man with a menial job but a powerful sense of vocation, and the menial job had somehow become the means by which he pursued his vocation. For, somehow, he knew that a street cleaner serves God by being a good street cleaner. Moreover, by his witness he unknowingly taught that lesson to hundreds of people by teaching it to me. For I, as a professional teacher, have passed it on to others to make part of their wisdom. A job, any job that serves a constructive purpose, even a menial job, has the meaning of a ministry; and by our faithfulness to it, we serve both God and man.[3]

Alan Richardson

After the idea of work as the creative activity of God, we find also in the Bible—and this is the most frequent usage of the word—the notion of man's ordinary, everyday, routine labour, by which he earns his daily bread. It is the kind of work which never comes to an end, like sowing and reaping, cooking and cleaning. It is the work without which men could not be fed and clothed and kept healthy, and without which society could not be ordered or cities inhabited. Work in this routine sense is regarded as the normal, fitting and inevitable lot of mankind. That man should work is as much a part of the regular order of things as that the sun should rise or that lions should hunt: 'man goeth forth to his work and to his labour until the evening' (Ps. 104.19-23). The prudential morality of the Wisdom Books is full of exhortations to industry and warnings against idleness. 'Go to the ant, thou sluggard; consider her ways, and be wise' (Prov. 6.6).

. . . .

The teaching of the Old Testament on the subject of work may be generally summed up by saying that it is regarded as a necessary and indeed God-appointed function of human life. Since to labour is the common lot of mankind, it is important that men should accept it without complaining and thus fulfil with cheerful obedience the intention of the Creator for human existence: 'Hate not laborious work, neither husbandry, which the Most High hath ordained' (Ecclus. 7.15). The basic assumption of the biblical viewpoint is that work is a divine *ordinance* for the life of man. As such it falls within the sphere of *law*—of God's requirement from man.

. . . .

When we have understood this, we shall not be surprised to find that in the New Testament the word 'work' as used of men

[3] Howe: *The Creative Years* (New York: The Seabury Press, 1959), pp. 179, 180, 182. Used by permission.

generally means something other than daily toil. A glance at a
concordance will shew that the word is used in the New Testament usually in indirect or quasi-metaphorical senses. Man's chief
'work' is not really *man's* work at all, but God's. The very faith of
believers is called the work of God: 'this is the work of God, that
ye believe on him whom he hath sent' (John 6.29; cf. Phil. 2.13;
II Thess. I.II). All our 'works'—that is, in biblical usage, our deeds,
thoughts, prayers, worship, service, faith—in so far as they are
good at all, are strictly the effects of God's working within us.
At most we co-operate with God and allow him to work through
us. Thus we become 'fellow-workers' with God (I Cor. 3.9; II Cor.
6.1; Mark 16.20).

.   .   .   .

The New Testament does not refer to 'vocation' in the modern
sense of a secular 'profession' or 'avocation'. In the New Testament
'vocation' (*klēsis*, 'calling') means God's call to repentance and
faith and to a life of fellowship and service in the Church. The
Bible knows no instance of a man's being called to an earthly
profession or trade by God. St. Paul, for example, is called by
God to be an apostle; he is not 'called' to be a tent-maker. It is
hardly too much to say that the Bible is uninterested in the various
professions and occupations in which men engage for the sake
of earning a livelihood, provided that they are honest; the standpoint of the Bible in general is that of John the Baptist's advice
to the tax-gatherers and soldiers in Luke 3.13f. In the course of his
parables our Lord makes reference to many occupations, from
those of kings or merchants to those of bailiffs or shepherds or
housewives, but he lets fall no comment upon the comparative
worth of any of these secular employments as such. Those whom
God calls (in the New Testament sense of the word) are summoned to 'work' within the Church, in the distinctive New Testament sense of the word 'work' which we have noted. They thus
become Christian 'workers' whatever may be their secular occupation.

Herein for the Christian lies the redemption of work. When a
man turns to Christ in repentance and faith, his whole life is

sanctified, including his life as a worker. What had formerly been done as sheer necessity, or perhaps out of a sense of duty, or even as a means of self-expression and fulfilment, is now done 'unto the Lord', and becomes joyous and free service and the source of deep satisfaction. 'A servant with this clause makes drudgery divine'—George Herbert's lines, hackneyed though they have become, express a truth of Christian experience which cannot be gainsaid. It is the task of the theologian to attempt to formulate in coldly intellectual prose the meaning of this experience, and any such attempted formulation will sound abstract and theoretical.[4]

Alexander Miller

While most of us have been growing up, there has been serious and hampering confusion, even among Christians, about the meaning of Christian faith and duty. There is a good deal of it still, but one of the hopeful signs in the world Church is that there is a growing number of things about which we agree. For one thing, there is common consent that the claim of Christ is a total claim. We are through with the idea that Christianity is a purely *spiritual* affair and our loyalty to Christ a purely *spiritual* loyalty. We know that, if the claim of Christ is valid, it is valid over the whole of life—over life both private and public, spiritual and material, economic and political.

.   .   .   .

For one of the most basic and "permanent" decisions we make is about the kind of job we do. Our choice of job conditions our whole life course, and any serious acceptance of the claim of Christ will mean that we let him choose our job for us. But even when we come to the point of accepting his right to do this, the actual working out of our obedience is far from easy in our day. Some jobs look as if they open a straight Christian course for us; with others it is very difficult to see how they can be called service of Christ at all. Whether or not this problem is peculiarly difficult

---

[4] Richardson, *The Biblical Doctrine of Work* (London: SCM Press Ltd., 1952), pp. 21, 23, 33, 35, 49.

in twentieth-century society, it is acute enough to make a grave problem of conscience for Christian men."[5]

Robert Lowry Calhoun

Vocation means being summoned or called. The inquiring mind will ask at once: "Being called to what and by whom?" Now just how is the answer to be given? Without a clear word on these matters, the mere statement that we are "called" becomes dry in our mouths. The answer proposed here to the question, "What are you going to do?" is stated in terms of another: "What does the God and Father of Jesus Christ bid us do? What has the burst of life that sprang from Galilee and that today encircles the globe to say on this everlastingly urgent problem? What is Christian vocation, for the men and women of our time?" . . . If every Christian is divinely summoned, he is called upon to act. His mission may or may not be the work of the Christian missionary, in the technical sense. That work needs many a community of burden-bearers. However repetitious his work may be, it remains an important projection of his inner being. As a person, he sees each job in terms of a whence and a whither; it is a step in a journey that has a beginning and an end. The meaning of work is contingent upon the laborer's purpose in life; the validity of the work rests first of all upon the validity of that purpose. Therefore, according to the Bible every work is dependent upon its hidden origins in the decisions of the workers.

> Unless the Lord builds the house,
> Those who build it labor in vain.
> Unless the Lord watches over the city,
> The watchman stays awake in vain. Ps. 127:1

. . . .

How, then, does the Bible view work? As an expression, an embodiment, of the worker's choices. Why is work significant? Because it is so closely tied up with the heart. The heart is really located where its treasures are. The work of the hands is a visible

[5] Miller, *Christian Faith and My Job*, (New Haven: Edward W. Hazen Foundation, Inc., 1946), pp. xi, xii, xiii.

pointer to that location, a signpost, however, that God alone can read. God influences man's work by addressing his heart, but the road to his heart often lies through his work. In confronting the heart of the worker through his work God invests that work with awesome significance. In responding to God through his work, a person determines the destiny of his heart. Heart and work are inseparable. Inseparable, also, although not interchangeable, are the purposes of man and the purposes of God. We must look then more closely at this relationship by giving attention to how God works through the worker.

The God of the Bible is pre-eminently a worker. In the idiom of the Psalm He is a builder of houses and a guardian of cities. He has done many marvelous things, is now doing them, and will soon complete them. From Him, through Him, and unto Him are all things. His activity embraces a wider universe than man's, yet He has chosen to seek the realization of His central purposes through this creature of dust. He intended that man should exercise dominion over other creatures. Through sin this dominion has been seriously perverted and curtailed. Yet God seeks its restoration. This will come about when in all of man's free activities God's sovereign purposes are realized. Until that day, man's labor tells a sorry story of defeat and destruction. Yet even the most terrible works of destruction shout a marvelous praise of the one true God. Even the collapse of houses points to His glorious power, though He intends the construction by human hands of houses that will weather every storm. His work thus precedes, interpenetrates, and either destroys or confirms the work of men's hands.

We must underscore this axiomatic outlook of the Bible. God is at work everywhere, and His work touches the work of man at innumerable points. He gives to the craftsman his artistry and cunning (Exod. 35:35). If the artisan achieves success he cannot say that it is solely due to his own skill, more workers, and for many Christians the divine summons will lead in that specific direction. But what is still more fundamental is that every Christian, rich or poor, ignorant or educated, Western or Eastern, has his mission in the world, his vocation that no one but he can fulfil. To find that mission and to act in line with it is vital for his personal well-being. It is vital also, as far as the life of an individual can be, for the well-being of his family, his nation, and his world. . . . Our lives have fallen apart because we have lost sight of the meaning of worship and work.

Worship as here understood is an experience in which man finds himself confronted by reality so great or so good, or both, that he stands in awe of it; yet reality with which, through some mediation, he finds himself reconciled or brought into communion and to which he commits his life without misgiving. From the first stage of such experience to the last, faith is involved—belief in the real presence of the Other, trust in its power and goodness, and self-devotion to its service. The normal issue of such devotion is active work, guided by the insight that worship brings. Worships and devout work together make up religious living. When they are split apart or flattened out, religion and life both suffer. . . .

If this is true, we may legitimately ask a question: "Is not this work that man must do itself part and parcel of the very process of creation and redemption in which God is continually engaged, and as such does it not embody a divine demand upon men?" In other words, is it not reasonable to ask whether the perpetual summons to work is not itself a summons from God to man, a divine vocation or calling (in principle alike for all men, although in specific ways different for each), through which God's task of creation and the process of overcoming and eradicating evil finds an essential part of its accomplishment? If the answer to this question is "Yes," then it would seem reasonable further to regard man as divinely called to nothing less than an actual part, though a minor and dependent one, in God's own perpetual task of making and remaking his world. Saint Paul's word, "For we are God's co-workers" (I Corinthians 3.9), would then have the most literal and tremendous meaning for our daily living.[6]

[6] Calhoun, *God and the Day's Work* (New York: Association Press, 1943), pp. v, vi, 8, 36, 37. Used by permission.

Paul S. Minear

Throughout the Bible it is the person who works to whom most attention is given, rather than the form or conditions of his work. A man works because of certain hopes and fears. By working, he surrenders some desires in order to fulfill others. By working, he gives voice to certain loyalties and obligations, taking his place in wisdom or power (Deut. 8:17, 18). God brings "forth food from the earth" (Ps. 104:14). All natural and human resources are from Him, not simply in terms of some long-ago act of creation but also in terms of continuous creation, sustenance, and purposeful guidance.[7]

Randolph Crump Miller

Vocation is work, but it is more. It is also man's total response to God in the situation in which he finds himself. . . .

The Gospel provides a framework for one's vocation, but the framework is of attitudes and relationships rather than of specific duties. . . .

The vocation of the Christian in the Church is to respond in faith to the grace of God vouchsafed in Jesus Christ. . . .

The response of faith also involves man's daily work. He is called to use the aptitudes that God has given him and that he has developed in the service of his fellow man. Part of the Church's mission is to make it possible for a society to use a man's real abilities for the well-being of that society. The individual must be the judge of whether his particular occupation meets these standards. No longer is there the contamination of idol worship or worship of the Emperor, but there are more subtle forces at work in many of today's jobs. Besides the forces of secularism and materialism which undercut many work opportunities, there is also a certain social snobbery in many vocational conferences for young people. They talk at great length about the ministry and other professions, with a side glance at parent-

[7] Minear: "Work and Vocation in Scripture" from *Work and Vocation,* edited by John Oliver Nelson (New York: Harper & Brothers, 1954), pp. 40, 43, 44. Used by permission.

hood, but say very little about the Christian opportunities of those at work in factories and mines.[8]

Carl Michalson

The Protestant Reformation helped to make it clear to Christians who were pouring their lives into their daily work that their life of faith was not suspended during working hours. Their vocational life was the arena in which God's calling was to be worked out. The consequence of that perspective was a repristination of work as divinely significant, a concept of the worker not as the victim of evil but as a steward in God's garden.

.   .   .   .

One who understands himself vocationally as in the image of God will adopt several attitudes of crucial importance to his well-being as a worker. For one thing, he will understand *the essential democracy of all vocations*. The dignity of work does not inhere in the nature of the work. Therefore, people cannot enhance their sense of self-esteem by comparing jobs. The dignity of work inheres in the way in which God is related to the work. As Martin Luther has said, every kind of work has its necessity and meaning in "the command of God." And as Calvin concurred, we are to do everything including our work for the glory of God.[9]

[8] Miller: *Biblical Theology and Christian Education* (New York: Charles Scribner's Sons, 1956), pp. 170, 171, 178. Used by Permission.
[9] Michalson, *Faith for Personal Crises* (New York: Charles Scribner's Sons, 1958), pp. 105, 106.

Appendix III

Sources of Referral on Vocational Problems

Throughout this study we have stressed the need for referral and interprofessional co-operation in all cases that would indicate it. We mentioned most of these agencies at one point or another in the discussion. This is not an attempt to describe them, but to list those agencies that are the major sources of referral on vocational matters.

Public Schools usually have a program of mental and vocational testing. Larger schools have counselors and guidance workers to do vocational counseling. Smaller schools depend on teachers and administrative personnel for such counseling.

Colleges and *Universities* provide vocational guidance and vocational testing. They often have files of occupational information and provide placement services for students. Placement services find part time employment for students and make contacts for placement of graduating seniors. Individual professors can provide guidance related to specific professions or special areas of work.

The United States Employment Service operates offices in every state providing jobs, vocational testing, information as to occupational trends, etc.

Private Employment Agencies provide jobs for clients on a fee basis.

Industrial Personnel Departments. Most large industrial firms provide guidance through their personnel departments. This is usually in relation to their own industries, but they do utilize aptitude testing and counseling.

Psychiatrists and *Psychologists* can be utilized when a vocational problem results in serious emotional disturbance as when a vocational problem seems to be the symptom of a major personality problem. Psychologists also give vocational tests along with other psychological tests.

The Veterans Administration works in the field of occupational therapy and vocational rehabilitation and provides social services for veterans.

The Office of Vocational Rehabilitation provides counseling, testing, and placement for the physically and mentally handicapped.

Goodwill Industries of America, Inc., provide employment for the handicapped.

Services for the Blind provide educational and vocational guidance and training for the blind.

The National Urban League helps locate jobs for Negroes.

B'nai B'rith provides vocational guidance for Jewish youth.

Rescue Missions and the *Salvation Army* provide jobs for transients, usually short term in nature.

The Y.M.C.A., Y.W.C.A. in some cities operate vocational guidance service.

The Public Library can be a valuable source of occupational information. Many libraries will order special material when it is requested.

Bibliography

American Personnel and Guidance Association. *Directory of Vocational Counseling Services, 1958-60.* Washington, D. C.: The Association, 1958.

Baer, Max F. and Roeber, Edward C. *Occupational Information: Its Nature and Use,* 2nd ed. Chicago: Science Research Associates, 1958. 495 pages.

Borow, Henry, and Lindsey, R. V. *Vocational Planning for College Students.* Englewood Cliffs, N. J.: Prentice-Hall, Inc., 1959. 186 pages.

Brewer, John M., and Others. *History of Vocational Guidance.* New York: Harper & Brothers, 1942. 344 pages.

————, and Landy, Edward. *Occupations Today,* new ed. Boston: Ginn & Company, 1956. 382 pages.

Burt, Jesse C. *Your Vocational Adventure.* New York: Abingdon Press, 1959. 203 pages.

Calhoun, Robert L. *God and the Day's Work.* New York: Association Press, 1943. 74 pages.

Crow, Lester D., and Crow, A. V. *Introduction to Guidance.* New York: American Book Company, 1951. 430 pages.

Ferrari, Erma Paul. *Careers for You.* New York: Abingdon Press, 1953. 160 pages.

Gilbert, Jeanne. *Understanding Old Age.* New York: Ronald Press, 1952. 422 pages.

Greenleaf, Walter James. *Occupations and Careers.* New York: McGraw-Hill Book Company, 1955. 605 pages.

Hoppock, Robert. *Occupational Information: Where to Get It and How to Use It in Counseling and Teaching.* New York: McGraw-Hill Book Co., 1957. 534 pages.

Horrocks, John E. *The Psychology of Adolescence*. Boston: Houghton Mifflin Company, 1951. 614 pages.

Humphreys, J. A., Traxler, A. E., and North, R. D. *Guidance Services*, rev. ed. Chicago: Science Research Associates, 1960. 432 pages.

Jones, Arthur J. *Principles of Guidance*. New York: McGraw-Hill Book Company, 1945. 592 pages.

Kuhlen, Raymond G. *Psychology of Adolescent Development*. New York: Harper & Brothers, 1952. 675 pages.

Lofquist, Lloyd H. *Vocational Counseling with the Physically Handicapped*. New York: Appleton-Century-Crofts Co., 1957. 384 pages.

McKinney, Fred. *Counseling for Personal Adjustment*. Boston: Houghton Mifflin Company, 1958. 584 pages.

Miller, Alexander. *Christian Faith and My Job*. New York: Association Press, 1946. 60 pages.

Myers, George E. *Principles and Techniques of Vocational Guidance*. New York: McGraw-Hill Book Company, 1941. 377 pages.

————, and Others. *Planning Your Future*, 4th ed. New York: McGraw-Hill Book Company, 1953. 526 pages.

Nelson, John Oliver. *Opportunities in Protestant Religious Vocations*. New York: Vocational Guidance Manuals, 1952.

————, ed. *Work and Vocation*. New York: Harper & Brothers, 1954. 224 pages.

Parsons, Frank. *Choosing a Vocation*. Boston: Houghton Mifflin Company, 1909.

Richardson, Alan. *The Biblical Doctrine of Work*. London: S.C.M. Press Ltd., 1952.

Rogers, Carl R. *Counseling and Psychotherapy*. Boston: Houghton Mifflin Company, 1942. 450 pages.

Rothney, J. W. M., and Roens, B. A. *Guidance of American Youth.* Cambridge: Harvard University Press, 1950. 269 pages.

Sanderson, Herbert. *Basic Concepts in Vocational Guidance.* New York: McGraw-Hill Book Co., 1954. 338 pages.

Science Research Associates. *Handbook of Job Facts,* 2nd ed. Chicago: Science Research Associates, 1959. 160 pages.

Shartle, Carroll Leonard. *Occupational Information; Its Development and Application,* 3rd ed. Englewood Cliffs, N. J.: Prentice-Hall, Inc., 1959. 384 pages.

Southard, Samuel. *Counseling for Church Vocations.* Nashville: Broadman Press, 1957. 126 pages.

Strang, Ruth. *The Adolescent Views Himself.* New York: McGraw-Hill Book Company, 1957. 581 pages.

Strong, Edward K., Jr. *Vocational Interests of Men and Women.* Stanford: Stanford University Press, 1943. 746 pages.

Super, Donald E. *The Psychology of Careers.* New York: Harper & Brothers, 1957. 362 pages.

————, and Others. *Vocational Development; a Framework for Research.* New York: Teachers College, Columbia University, 1957. 142 pages.

Thorndike, Robert L., and Hagen, E. P. *Ten Thousand Careers.* New York: John Wiley & Sons, 1959. 346 pages.

Traxler, Arthur E. *Techniques of Guidance.* New York: Harper & Brothers, 1945. 394 pages.

Trueblood, D. Elton. *Your Other Vocation.* New York: Harper & Brothers, 1952. 125 pages.

U. S. Department of Labor. Bureau of Labor Statistics, in cooperation with Veterans Administration. *Occupational Outlook Handbook.* Washington, D. C.: Superintendent of Documents, 1959. 800 pages.

U. S. Employment Service. *Dictionary of Occupational Titles.* Washington, D. C.; Superintendent of Documents.

Westervelt, Virginia V. *Choosing a Career in a Changing World.* New York: G. P. Putnam's Sons, 1960. 160 pages.

Williamson, E. G. *How to Counsel Students.* New York: McGraw-Hill Book Company, 1939. 562 pages.

The Personnel and Guidance Journal. Nine issues annually. Washington, D. C.: American Personnel and Guidance Association.

Occupational Briefs. Chicago: Science Research Associates.

Index

Ability, mental, 30f.
 tests of, 43f., 47
Adolescence, 43
Advantages in counseling
 of pastor, 118ff.
 of vocational counselor, 122ff.
Alcoholic, the, 158f.
Aptitude tests, 64
Army Alpha and Beta tests, 167
Avocations, 111f.

Beers, Clifford, 43, 166
Binet, Alfred, 43, 165f.
Bingham, Walter, 65
Bloomfield, Meyer, 167
B'nai B'rith Hillel Foundation, 45,
 168, 182
*Book of Trends or Library of the
 Useful Arts, The*, 74
Breadwinners' Institute, 37, 43, 46,
 166
Brewer, John M., 35ff., 48, 49
Brooks, Superintendent of Boston
 schools, 40f.
Brunner, Emil, 171
Buehler, Charlotte, 28

Calhoun, Robert Lowry, 176ff.
California Mental Maturity tests, 57
Choice of vocation, 23f., 30, 33, 50
 importance of, 11ff.
 past versus present, 40
 questions for, 77-80
 satisfaction in, 104ff.
Choosing a Vocation, 37f., 47, 166
Chronological chart, 165ff.

Church
 and the handicapped, 151
 relation to vocational guidance,
  50, 101ff.
Church vocations, 115ff.
 denominational differences, 120
 principles of counseling in, 129-
  133
 recruitment for, 130
 training for, 121
 try-out opportunities, 121f.
Cincinnati, 41
Civic Service House of Boston, 37
Client-centered approach, 48, 55f.
Committee on vocational advice, 41
Concept of "self," 25
 understanding of, 26
Crow and Crow, 41
Cumulative record, 48

Dangers of testing, 66f.
Decline, 29
Department of the Blind, 154
*Dictionary of Occupational Titles,
 The*, 40, 46, 75, 168, 169
Directive approach, 48, 55f.

Educational guidance, 27f., 41f.
 first use of the term, 42
 of the handicapped, 154
Emotions, 13, 22, 44
 discouragement, 31, 104f., 110
 embarrassment, 31
 failure, 110
 frustration, 31, 104f., 139
 with the handicapped, 156

Employment Managers' Association,
    45
Establishment stage, 29
Ex-convict, the, 158f.
Exploratory stage, 29

General Aptitude Test Battery, 65
Gifted, the, 147ff.
Gilbert, Jeanne, 138f.
Gillespie, James, 147
Goodwill Industries of America,
    Inc., 154, 165, 182
Grand Rapids Department of Vo-
    cational Guidance, 41, 167
Greene, H. A., 34
Greenleaf, Walter James, 60
Growth stage, 28f.

Hall, G. Stanley, 43
Handicapped, the, 46, 56, 126,
    150-158
  degree of handicap, 152
  referral agencies, 154
  spiritual needs of, 157
Harner, Nevin, 96f.
Hazen, Edward, 36, 165
Henmon-Nelson test, 57
Horrocks, John E., 27, 31
Howe, Reuel L., 171f.
Humphreys and Traxler, 95

Index of Occupations, 75
Interests tests, 61f.
Interview, 54f.
IQ tests, 57

Job satisfaction, 105ff.
Jones, Arthur J., 44

Kelley, Truman, 42, 167
Kuder Preference Record, 48, 61f.,
    168
Kuhlen, Raymond G., 73f.

Life Stages, 28-30
Literature
  A Vocational Guidance News-
      Letter, 47, 166
  An Enlistment Manual for
      Church Vocations, 116
  Occupational Fields in Protestant
      and Orthodox Churches, 115
  Occupational Guides, 76
  Occupational Outlook Handbook,
      76
  Occupations, 47, 168
  The Personnel and Guidance
      Journal, 47, 169
  Vocational Guidance Magazine,
      47, 167

Maintenance stage, 29
McKinney, Fred, 58
Mental ability, 30f.
Mental hygiene movement, 43f.,
    166
Mental measurement movement,
    43f, 57
Mental patient, 158f.
Mental tests, 43f., 47, 57ff.
Merrill, George A., 36, 165
Michalson, Carl, 180
Miller, Alexander, 175
Miller, Randolph Crump, 179
Mind that Found Itself, A, 43
Minear, Paul, 179
Ministers' responsibility in counsel-
    ing, 92ff.
Movements
  mental hygiene, 43f.
  mental measurement, 43f., 57
  pastoral counseling, 51
  religious education, 51
  vocational guidance, 43ff., 57
Myers, George, 122

National Rehabilitation Association, 46, 168
National Urban League, 45, 166, 182
National Vocational Guidance Association, 46, 50, 168
Nelson, John Oliver, 115, 116, 126

Oakland, 41
Occupational information, 80-84, 168
Occupational Information and Guidance Service, 46
Occupations 47, 168
Office of Vocational Rehabilitation, 85f., 154f., 182
Ohio State University Psychological Examination, 57
Older persons, 128
    principles for working with, 138-141
Otis Quick-Scoring Test, 57

Panorama of Professions and Trades, The, 36
Parsons, Frank, 35, 36f., 41f., 45, 47, 166
    principles of counseling, 38
Pastoral counseling movement, 51
Pastor as counselor, 33, 102ff., 109
    for the retarded, 142f.
    in church vocations, 117f.
    in retirement, 136f.
    of the handicapped, 152
Personal feelings, 32f.
Personality tests, 65f.
Personnel and Guidance Journal, The, 47, 169
Principles of counseling
    for church vocations, 129-133
    Parsons, 38
    with convicts, alcoholics, etc., 159-161

Principles of counseling—*Continued*
    with retired persons, 138-141
    with the gifted, 148-150
    with the handicapped, 153-158
    with the retarded, 143-147
Principles of testing, 68-72
Problems, 22, 92f., 102ff.
    in counseling for church vocations, 125ff.
    of the retarded, 142f.
Psychoanalysis
    development of, 44
Psychology of Careers, 47
Public schools, 39f., 181

Questions for vocational choice, 77-80

Recruitment for church vocations, 130
Religious education movement, 51
Retarded, the, 56, 142f.
    extent of retardation, 143f.
    vocations for, 145f.
Retirement, 135ff.
Richards, Lysander, 36, 165
Richardson, Alan, 173ff.
Rogers, Carl, 55, 168
Rorschach ink blot test, 65f.
Ross, C. C., 59
Rothney and Roens, 45
Rupert, Hoover, 97

Sanderson, Herbert, 22f., 35
Seashore Measures of Musical Talent, 64f., 167
Shartle, Carroll Leonard, 73, 168
Spann, J. Richard, 97
Stanford-Binet, 57
Stenquist Mechanical Ability Test, 64f., 167
Strang, Ruth, 32f.

Strong, Edward K., Jr., 48, 61f.
Strong Vocational Interest Inventory, 48
Super, Donald, 28, 47, 108
Switzer and Rusk, 155

Tests
  Army Alpha, 167
  Army Beta, 167
  California Mental Maturity, 57
  educational achievement, 58ff.
  General Aptitude Test Battery, 65
  group, 57
  Henmon-Nelson, 57
  individual, 57
  IQ, 57
  mental, 43f., 47
  Ohio State University Psychological Examination, 57
  Otis Quick-Scoring Test, 57
  performance, 58
  personality, 65
  Seashore Measures of Musical Talent, 64f.
  special tests, 58
  Stanford-Binet, 57
  Stenquist Mechanical Ability Test, 64f.
  Strong Vocational Interest Inventory, 48
  Thematic Apperception test, 66
  vocational aptitude, 60
  vocational interest, 60
  Vocational Preference Record, 48
  Wechsler-Bellevue Scale, 57
Thematic Apperception Test, 66
Thorndike, Edward L., 43
Transient, the, 158f.

Traxler, Arthur, 41f.
Trueblood, Elton, 96

United States Employment Service, 46, 65, 76, 85, 154, 167, 181

Values of testing, 67f.
Veterans' Administration, 154, 182
Vocaphy, 36, 165
Vocation
  choice of, 11ff., 23f., 30, 33, 106
  glamor in, 26, 61, 111
  nature of, 26
  questions, 77-80
Vocational adjustment, 101f.
  of the handicapped, 151f.
Vocational guidance, 27, 33f., 41f.
  as a career, 21, 46
  changing emphases, 49
  first use of term, 35, 166
  in church vocations, 117f.
  in public schools, 39f.
  movement, 165ff.
  need for, 40
  training for, 47
Vocational Guidance Magazine, 47, 167
Vocational guidance movement, 43ff., 57
Vocational Guidance News-Letter, A, 47, 166
Vocational Preference Record, 48
Vocation Bureau of Boston, 35, 37

Warters, Jane, 95
Wechsler-Bellevue Scale, 57
Whitehead, Alfred North, 34
Williamson, E. G., 48, 55
YMCA, 45, 77, 86, 166, 182